CLARENDON LIBRARY OF LOGIC AND PHILOSOPHY

General Editor: L. Jonathan Cohen

ONTOLOGICAL ECONOMY

ALSO PUBLISHED IN THIS SERIES

The Probable and the Provable by L. Jonathan Cohen

Relative Identity by Nicholas Griffin

Experiences: An Inquiry into some Ambiguities by J. M. Hinton

Knowledge by Keith Lehrer

The Cement of the Universe: A Study of Causation by J. L. Mackie

Truth, Probability and Paradox by J. L. Mackie

The Nature of Necessity by Alvin Plantinga

Divine Commands and Moral Requirements by P. L. Quinn

Simplicity by Elliott Sober

The Coherence of Theism by Richard Swinburne

The Emergence of Norms by Edna Ullmann-Margalit

Ignorance: A Case for Scepticism by Peter Unger

Metaphysics and the Mind-Body Problem by Michael E. Levin

ONTOLOGICAL ECONOMY: SUBSTITUTIONAL QUANTIFICATION AND MATHEMATICS

DALE GOTTLIEB

OXFORD UNIVERSITY PRESS
1980

Oxford University Press, Walton Street, Oxford OX2 6DP

OXFORD LONDON GLASGOW
NEW YORK TORONTO MELBOURNE WELLINGTON
KUALA LUMPUR SINGAPORE JAKARTA HONG KONG TOKYO
DELHI BOMBAY CALCUTTA MADRAS KARACHI
NAIROBI DAR ES SALAAM CAPE TOWN

© *Dale Gottlieb 1980*

Published in the United States
by Oxford University Press, New York

British Library Cataloguing in Publication Data

Gottlieb, Dale
  Ontological economy – (Clarendon library of logic and philosophy).
  1. Ontology
  I. Title
  111 BD331 79-41318
  ISBN 0-19-824420-7

Printed in Great Britain by
Spottiswoode Ballantyne Ltd., Colchester and London

Preface

Since chapter I is devoted to a survey of the topics included in this book and their background, I will say here just that the first part gives an account of ontological commitment and substitutional quantification in a broad philosophical setting, and the second part attempts to construct an ontologically neutral language for at least the lower reaches of mathematics. Although logicians' symbols encroach upon even the first part at various points, an effort has been made to describe the underlying motivation for the various positions so that the discussion is accessible to anyone with an interest in formal semantics, systematic ontology, theory reduction, and related topics. My experience indicates that graduate students with a couple of semesters of logic can read it from cover to cover.

Some of the central themes of this project first appeared in "Reference and Ontology", "A Method for Ontology, with Applications to Numbers and Events" *Journal of Philosophy*, 1974, 1976), "The Truth About Arithmetic" (*American Philosophical Quarterly*, 1978), and "The Concepts of Validity and Logical Truth for Languages with Substitutional Quantification" (to appear in the inaugural issue of *Idea*). Material from those papers is used here by permission of the publishers.

Many teachers, colleagues and students have provided invaluable stimuli for my philosophical thinking. John Vickers and Jean van Heijenoort introduced me to philosophical logic. Nelson Goodman and W. V. O. Quine—the former through his lectures at Brandeis University, and both through their writings—have set the "paradigm" within which the research in this book is conducted. Larry Davis, Peter Achinstein, and especially Robert Cummins were inexhaustible sources of suggestion and critique. Finally, of most relevance to this book was Timothy McCarthy; everything save the last two chapters was exhaustively discussed between us. Without his collaboration this book would not be.

The first draft of this book was written in Jerusalem in the spring of 1977 while I was on a sabbatical leave from the Johns Hopkins

University, which support I gratefully acknowledge. From my parents, parents-in-law, wife, and children came constant encouragement and aid in all forms, without which work would have been impossible. Finally, to the Source of life and all blessings, I can only respond: "Though my mouth were filled with song like the sea, I could not begin to acknowledge even one of Your myriad lovingkindnesses."

D.V.G.

Contents

Part I: Method

Part II: Application

Part I

Method

I

Introduction

Contemporary philosophy abounds with tightly constructed, clearly presented arguments for middle-sized theses. The theses are theory-laden—"Possible-world semantics for counterfactuals", "Arithmetic is synthetic *a priori*", "Functional states of the brain are not mental states"—and the arguments tend to be framed in, or make essential appeal to, formal languages whose semantics and syntax are (supposedly) precise. All this is to be applauded. Much argument at cross purposes is avoided, and some conclusions can be established firmly so that philosophy does not perennially describe a circle. Common theories create enough mutual understanding to allow communities of philosophers to co-ordinate their efforts in developing those theories to the extent of their powers.

Nevertheless, something more is needed to give motivation and direction to such theses and their arguments. They are relevant because they are attempts to understand and apply theories which are incomparably deeper in their foundations and broader in their applications than the middle-sized theses themselves. If the theories are not clearly in view, arguments tend to be conducted in a vacuum. It is unclear why a particular thesis is important and what the consequences are of its truth or falsity. We may even become somewhat unsure of our standards of relevance for arguments pro and con. It seems to me, therefore, that it is incumbent upon a philosopher to make clear his deepest theoretical orientation and commitments, especially when his mode of argument is largely in or about formal languages. But this is hard to do, for two reasons. First not everyone who works in formal philosophy *has* an integrated deep theory which defines his overall approach. Second, even one who has will find it very difficult to define it precisely, present it in an organized way, and argue for it convincingly. Thus one's deepest philosophy tends to be an unspoken premiss of all of one's work, one which is divined (or not) by the subtle, well-trained reader, and often a mystery to the uninitiate. Who, after all, wants to publicly subscribe to an ill-defined, disorganized, and poorly defended bunch of intuitions and tout it as his deepest philosophy?

This Introduction is an attempt to escape the dilemma. Here I will present the intuitions which are my starting points for the middle-sized theses to be defined and defended in the later chapters. I will not define them precisely or defend them because I cannot do so. Even so, the reader has a right to know my basic outlook so that he can have some perspective on the detailed arguments to follow. What follow are six clusters of such intuitions, together with the theses of later chapters to which they are most relevant.

1. *Language is a describer and recorder of reality, not its creator. Theory of language may commit us to a view concerning the nature of certain facets of the world, but that view will be tested in the way that all theoretical posits are tested—by its ability to contribute to an explanation of the phenomena for which the theory is responsible.*
Language is part of our general project of symbolizing reality; it is one symbol system among many whose purpose is to enable us to represent the world and thus think about it and understand it. As a medium of representation and thought, language reflects and can create constraints on how we understand the world. Our most basic categories as expressed by language may be more or less apt to produce an understandable model of the reality we experience. Still, it is possible—and crucial—to separate language from reality and to keep the reactive nature of language clearly in mind. The world calls the shots: it is as it is independently of how we think about it, and of what kinds of languages we devise to describe it. If our picture of the world is incoherent, this may be because we have an inaccurate or imcomplete picture of some of its parts, or because our language is barring us from describing it correctly. Improvement will come with more careful and thorough investigation and with improvement of our language. The one thing we cannot do is to adjust the contents of reality to fit the descriptive resources of our language. It will not do to "discover" or "posit" entities for the sole reason that, in talking about those facets of the world whose existence is not in question, we seem to mention the new entities as well. It is not a sufficient argument for infinitesimals that we mention them in the calculus which describes motion, nor for Aristotelian substances that we mention them in describing change, nor for propositions that we mention them in

describing belief. Likewise, it is not a sufficient argument for the existence of any (kind of) entity that in order to display the logical form of the sentences of our language we have to portray them as referring to that (kind of) entity. Analysis of logical form contributes to understanding *what our language commits us to*, but does not determine what there is. Thus Donald Davidson's "method of truth in metaphysics"[1] is rejected; the ontological presuppositions of my language are merely the outgrowths of my language and, once uncovered, must then be put to an independent test against reality.

The study of language is thus not the central strand in ontology. But the study of language does contribute its own theoretical commitments, as does the study of physics, the arts, psychology, and so on. Commitments engendered by the theory of truth have received the most attention to date. Truth is the resultant of language and the world: a sentence is true because of its truth conditions and because of the way the world is. The theory of truth must display the truth conditions of the sentences of our language and explain their function as truth conditions. The latter entails a description and explanation of how language and the world make contact. Referential semantics is a start: certain expressions (quantifiers, singular terms, and predicates) enjoy direct relations to entities, and on the basis of those direct relations the language-world tie of all sentences is to be explained. A needed supplement is the analysis of those direct semantical relations themselves. In its absence, we know only *where* the tie is *anchored* and *how on the side of language* it is transmitted to the infinity of sentences. Now it is precisely in the implementation of the referential programme for linking language to the world that theoretical posits may be needed. But the standard by which these posits will be judged is their overall contribution to our understanding of language—including the use of language: communication, thought, propositional attitudes, language learning, etc. Thus for example it will not do to argue that numbers and sets exist because of the logical connections holding among sentences which express the results of our countings ("there are n F's"), unless numbers and sets can contribute to our general theory of language.

Chapter III applies these reflections to the use of the criterion of ontological commitment in settling ontological disputes. Extreme conservatism and caution is urged: unless the entities which logical

---

[1] Davidson, 1977.

form and truth theory need can be integrated into an explanation of how language works (and into our general picture of the rest of the world), we must not "posit" them but rather reform our language. Conservatism is also a corollary of the availability of substitutional quantification with which logical form may at least sometimes be rendered without ontological commitment. The general conditions under which this is possible are discussed.

2. Language contacts reality through quantifiers. The ontological commitment of a theory is what it asserts with its existential quantifiers. Possible world semantics is unnecessary and misleading as an approach to ontological commitment.

Language abounds with expressions which look like singular terms and predicates, but which are used non-referring in a perfectly legitimate way. (Examples: 'the average taxpayer', 'the equator', 'the state', 'Zeus'; 'Ponce de Leon searched for x', 'x believes y', 'x is a picture of y'.) To pick out those terms (or: those uses of terms) which refer, we need an expression which is always used referringly. Referential use of other terms is then determined by their relation to the referential tell-tale. Quine chose the quantifiers as the constant symptom of reference and, on one interpretation, used logic to express the key relation: use of a term is referential iff that use logically implies an appropriate existential quantification. I accept this strategy, with one reservation. It is only the objectually interpreted quantifier which uniformly indicates reference. Since substitutional quantifiers are as much a part of our language as objectual quantifiers are, we cannot use expressions of ordinary language to announce reference unless we can distinguish the two interpretations of quantification in ordinary language. Quine apparently thinks we can distinguish, and I will not disagree. Thus referential use of a term is a use with objectual existentially quantified logical consequences.

In chapter II I argue that ontological commitment is a non-extensional feature of theories: it is their possessing the relevant theorems. Thus ontological commitment is explicated via objectual quantification and logical implication. The second component, being "intensional", invites other non-extensional alternatives. In particular, Michael Jubien replaces implication with necessity in terms of a possible world structure.[2] Ontological commitment becomes a relation

---

[2] Jubien, 1974.

between theories and possibilia. I find his theory unacceptable for three reasons. (1) Since the account in terms of implication is fully adequate, we do not need the highly suspicious possible worlds machinery to this end. (2) His account is inconsistent: he claims that the necessity he employs is logical necessity, but the use of his criterion belies this claim. (3) His crucial examples turn on a fundamentally mistaken application of possible world semantics: even if intensions can be represented as functions on possible worlds, there are more such functions than there are intensions to be represented. Jubien applies his criterion to functions which cannot represent the intensions of any terms, and hence that application cannot reveal the ontological commitments of any theory. When restricted to actual theories it appears that his criterion agrees with Quine's (as amended) and hence is superfluous.

3. *The semantical interpretation of a sentence is its truth condition. Semantics is the theory of truth conditions: how they are formulated and assigned, and the significance of thus interpreting sentences. (The latter enables semantics to tie in to psychology and thus help explain the use of language.) There are no a priori formal constraints on how truth conditions are assigned.*

I am attracted to realism in semantics—with Davidson and against Dummett. Thus I think of truth conditions as the prime candidates as meanings for sentences. Nevertheless, semantics must be no less than a complete theory of meaning: we must be able to explain everything that meanings are traditionally used to explain by appeal to truth conditions. A speaker's grasp of his language must be represented as his knowing the truth conditions of its sentences; truth conditions must give the content of propositional attitudes; truth conditions must be what the new speaker learns when he learns the language; and so on. I assume that this can be done, and hence am content to treat the semantical interpretation of a language as the assignment of truth conditions to its sentences.

The number and variety of theoretically central roles which truth conditions are expected to play provide strong constraints upon semantical interpretation. But there are no *a priori formal* constraints except that the assignment be effective. Unfortunately such constraints have become strongly associated with Davidsonian semantics. For example, the semantical and syntactical primitives are taken to coincide; the semantical interpretation of an expression is taken to be a function solely of the semantical interpretations of its (significant) parts; and the logical form of a sentence is taken to dictate its semantical interpretation. None of these generalizations is inherent in the idea of truth conditional semantics, and all of them are violated when we provide such a semantics for languages incorporating substitutional quantification. In such languages the relation between syntax and semantics is exceedingly complex; perhaps the best that can be said is that the syntactical structure of a sentence helps determine its truth conditions in the manner specified by the assignment: there may be no simple way to sum up the semantical role of syntactically primitive expressions. The semantical interpretation of a sentence will be a function of the semantical interpretations of its parts *and other expressions of the language*, and not solely of the former. And the logical form of a sentence, in so far as it is revealed by the schema associated with the sentence, may determine only a part of its semantic interpretation. Chapter IV describes these deviations from Davidsonian form in detail.

4. *Logic is the study of valid—i.e., formally truth-preserving—argument.*[3] *Logic provides a semantical theory which defines validity precisely and attempts to explain it. Logic also attempts to provide a practical procedure for identifying valid arguments, though this is only a hoped-for benefit of logical theory, not a criterion of its adequacy.*

In some arguments the guarantee of truth which the premisses provide the conclusion is due to their respective forms. Logic is the theory of such formal guarantees. By appeal to various semantically defined categories of expressions, form is defined precisely. The semantical interpretation of the "logical constants" then makes possible an explanation of the guarantee. (Thus, in a way, argumental validity is a linguistic guarantee of truth. It is possible to accept this and still agree with Quine that even logic is at bottom empirical if one thinks (as Quine does) that there is no clear line between revising belief and revising language. For then the revision of language—and hence the revision of logic—can be a response to empirical pressures.)

Validity is easiest to discern in a formal language, i.e., a language in which the syntactic structure of a sentence is a strong indicator of its

---

[3] This is the standard approach to logic; for the outline to a nominalist alternative, cf. chapter VI, section (3).

semantical interpretation. For such languages we may attempt to devise practical, mechanical procedures for determining validity. These calculi equate validity with some more or less effectively discoverable syntactic feature of the premisses and conclusion (and possibly other fixed features of the language). But there is nothing in the nature of validity itself to ensure that such calculi exist. It is a surprising result that they can sometimes be found.[4] Of course, that *some* valid arguments can be identified syntactically is a necessary feature of formal languages: in such languages the syntactic structure of a sentence is a strong enough indicator of its semantical interpretation to effectively determine many of its logical relations. But this does not guarantee a calculus which picks out only valid arguments and manages to get all of them. (It tends to be forgotten that neither Frege nor Russell even framed the question of completeness for their calculi.)

Therefore, the fact that a particular conception of validity is accompanied by a complete calculus has no weight in recommending that conception. I find Quine's complaint against branching quantifiers that they possess no complete proof procedure irrelevant; it is certainly no reason to replace them with quantifiers over functions.[5] Similarly, the fact that the semantics for substitutional quantification validates the omega-rule and thereby deprives languages with substitutional quantification of a complete proof procedure is no reason for concern. It is certainly no reason to use intuitively baseless artifices to redefine substitutional validity so as to restore completeness, as do Hintikka and LeBlanc;[6] in chapter V their approach is rejected for this reason. Also rejected is Kripke's attempt to marshal intuition against the validity of the omega-rule for substitutional semantics.[7] The result is that we embrace a formal logic which is incomplete, in much the same spirit that we accept the incompleteness of arithmetic.

It may be objected that to allow unrecognizable validity removes logic too far from its starting place, viz., arguments whose premisses guarantee their conclusions in such a way as to extend our knowledge. Logic is essentially an epistemic tool; "valid" arguments which can't be *seen* to be valid do not affect the usefulness of this tool. Now I agree wholeheartedly with this description of the function of valid

---

[4] Boolos, 1975, 523–4.
[5] Quine, 1973 [43], 90–1, and Boolos, 1975, 523.
[6] Davidson, 1973, 6.
[7] Kripke, 1976, 335–6.

argument. But logic must *explain* how valid arguments can perform this function. It does so by defining validity semantically and then—*voilà*—semantical validity turns out to be possessed by more arguments than we can ever know. This does not affect the conclusion that it is *this* feature which is epistemologically crucial in the arguments which we *do* know to possess it.

5. *Study of the semantics of first order languages contributes both to the development of a very useful, if limited, fragment of natural language, and ultimately to the understanding of natural language as a whole.*

There are two common positions concerning the significance of first order languages. The first is positive, holding that they are the only languages we really understand, and hence only they should be used. They admit of a completely extensional semantics, and a complete formal proof procedure, and the behavioural underpinnings of their primitive expressions are reasonably clear. Since this cannot be said for any importantly stronger formal language, let alone unformalized natural language, if we wish to understand what we are saying, we must say it in first-orderese. Unwillingness to so restrict one's discourse expresses a perverse love of obscurantism, or the inherent muddleheadedness of one's ideas.

The second position is negative, pointing out that to date, first order languages do not permit the expression of many notions which are indispensable to philosophy such as subjunctives, modals, deontics, etc. Furthermore, they claim that any understanding of language, either idealized and streamlined or the jungle of actually spoken language, will have to be rooted in the linguistic behaviour of speakers, and *they* don't speak a first order language. Restricting one's purview to first order languages shows a perverse disregard for the most significant and difficult problems in the philosophy of language.

In all likelihood, the truth lies in between. The limits of first order languages today may be only the limits of our ingenuity to date; there are precious few *proofs* of their *inherent* limitations. Some needed extensions may be allowed without compromising the philosophical programmes they serve—branching quantifiers and cardinality quantifiers are perhaps examples. Furthermore, the extent to which the extensional semantics for first order languages may *inspire* treatments of intensionality should not be forgotten. (Possible world semantics simply extends extensional semantics to a field of possible worlds; in other respects it is parallel to its forebear.) Finally, the study of the extensional semantics for first order languages may help us understand the nature of semantics in general. The significance of truth conditions as the basis of meaning, the recursive form of semantical interpretation, and the ultimate empirical significance of semantics are best studied first in the simplest case.

Thus all should agree that it is beneficial to develop the resources of first order languages to their fullest and that is what this book attempts with respect to the nominalization of mathematics. The goal is a semantics for the language of mathematics which is first order and eschews abstracta; its construction is described in Part II. Part I gives the semantical background, and in particular defines ontological commitment for such languages so that it may be clear what criteria should be employed in judging the success of that construction.

6. *Abstract entities are mysterious and must be avoided at all costs. They are especially pernicious in mathematics where they make understanding of the application of mathematics very unlikely, and hence cannot be part of acceptable truth conditions for the sentences of mathematics.*
It is a mystery how we concrete beings can know abstracta, and in general the possibility of interaction between abstracta and concreta is doubtful. In this respect properties, sets, rules, and so on are equally objectionable. Perhaps their mysteriousness is so damning that it is in principle forbidden to add them to our world view: since nothing can be explained through them (and much can be obscured), they are never successful as theoretical posits. Or perhaps they are not in principle unintelligible, but are just so undesirable that it is always easier to understand the world without them than with them. In either case, the less we use them the better.

Mathematics seems to be the discipline in strongest need of abstracta, and yet it seems to me that they do it more harm than good. Paul Benaceraff thinks that only abstracta can enable us to do justice to the semantics of mathematical language.[8] Michael Dummett and Michael Jubien argue to the contrary (and I agree) that it is unclear how reference, and hence any semantical relation, to abstracta can be achieved.[9] In addition, portraying the subject matter of mathematics

---

[8] Benaceraff, 1973.
[9] Dummett, 1973, chapter 14 and Jubien, 1977.

as the nature of numbers, functions, etc. makes it very difficult to explain how mathematical knowledge helps in comparing the results of counting concreta, tuning cars, building bridges, and understanding the physical world in which we live. This latter point affects semantics as well. For, one irreducible aspect of the mastery of the language of mathematics is the ability to apply the truths of "pure" mathematics to concrete situations. Thus in order for the semantics of mathematical language to help explain that mastery it must represent the meanings of mathematical sentences in a form which makes applicability clear. Again, abstracta are more a hindrance than a help.

In chapters VI and VII an account of the arithmetic of natural numbers and fractions is offered which is numberless. In addition, the acceptable axioms of arithmetic are logically true in the narrow sense of being roughly "infinite conjunctions" of first order tautologies. The result is a literal logicism for an arithmetic slightly weaker than usual, and that logicism has the metaphysical and epistemological benefits which older forms of logicism promised but could not deliver: freedom from ontological commitment to abstracta, and a reduction of the epistemological status of mathematics to that of logic. The weakness of the axioms is dictated by the semantics which takes applications of arithmetic to be fundamental for the truth conditions of mathematical sentences, and is justified from that standpoint. It is an open question how much more of traditional mathematics can be achieved by extending the account of rational arithmetic; a few sketchy remarks suggest the direction in which further development may be expected.

An account of mathematics which takes applications seriously must be responsible for the truth conditions of all sentences in which mathematical terms appear. In chapters VI and VII the application taken as paramount is the schema 'there are exactly n F's'; its instances are made the backbone of the truth conditions for sentences of rational arithmetic. Those sentences in turn receive truth conditions via familiar combinations of quantification and identity. But there are other applications—other contexts in which numerals appear and to which mathematical truths are applied. One such is measurement. Chapter VIII is an attempt to adapt at least one account of measurement to nominalist scruples. Truth conditions are suggested for measurement sentences such as "John is 6 feet tall" which require no reference to abstracta and to which the truths of arithmetic, understood in terms of the account of chapters VI and VII, can apply.

Ideally we should be able to make an exhaustive list of all the contexts in which numerals can occur and provide numberless truth conditions for all of them. Only then could we be *sure* that numbers are not needed. But I have no idea how to make such a list. So I have attempted here to deal with the most basic contexts in the hope that many others may be reducible to these, and that the techniques used here may prove fruitful for the remainder. If the objectives of chapters VI–VIII are met, the case for nominalism is greatly strengthened; to *establish* nominalism as completely satisfactory will have to wait for another effort.

II

The Non-Extensionality of Ontological Commitment

The goal of this chapter and the next is a criterion for ontological commitment. In order to state such a criterion precisely and test it we must have some understanding of this notion with which to start. We need to be able to identify clear cases of commitment, and we need to know something of its general nature. It is agreed that it is theories which incur ontological commitments directly; people inherit them from the theories they espouse. Controversy is focused around the question which is the subject of this chapter: Is ontological commitment a property of theories, or a relation? If the latter, to what are theories related by this commitment? I shall argue that (i) ontological commitment cannot be construed as a relation between theories and objects; (ii) an adequate account of ontological commitment may be had by construing it as an intra-linguistic property of theories; and (iii) the attempt by Michael Jubien to construe ontological commitment as a relation between theories and possibilia is unnecessary (by ii) and certain consequences of his theory of commitment are incorrect. As a result, a criterion due to Quine will be vindicated—until chapter III when its infirmities will come to light.

To ask whether ontological commitment is a property or a relation is to ask for the semantical analysis of sentences of the form: 'T is ontologically committed to a/F's' (to be called *OC sentences*), wherein 'T' is a slot for names of theories, and 'a' and 'F's' are schematic for singular terms and predicates respectively. In particular, are we to accord referential status to expressions in the 'a' slot and satisfaction status to the expressions in the 'F's' slot? There is one argument against so doing, which in my opinion is decisive. There are many sentences attributing ontological commitment which are true, and yet there are no entities referred to by the singular term replacing 'a', nor are there entities satisfying the predicate replacing 'F's'. For example,

(1) '$(\exists x)(x = \text{Zeus})$' is ontologically committed to Zeus

and

(2) ‘(∃x)(x is a unicorn)’ is ontologically committed to unicorns.

If, in the manner of traditional referential semantics, ‘Zeus’ is taken as a referring term in (1) and ‘unicorns’ as a predicate with extension in (2), then (1) and (2) cannot be true. For, (1) asserts a relation between the sentence ‘(∃x)(x = Zeus)’ and whatever is referred to by ‘Zeus’—it is on a par with ‘George is taller than Zeus’—and hence the fact that ‘Zeus’ has no referent prevents (1) from being true. The problem with (2) is similar, though in order to see it we have to construe (2) more explicitly: the syntactic role of the predicate ‘unicorns’ must be specified. The most natural construal is

(2a) (∃x)(x is a unicorn & ‘(∃x)(x is a unicorn)’ is ontologically committed to x).

But (2a) is false—its first conjunct fails due to the non-existence of unicorns—even though (2) is true. Thus the referential analysis of OC sentences fails.

Some wish to distinguish the question of the extensionality of OC sentences (i.e., of those formed by replacing ‘a’ with a singular term) from the question answered in the last paragraph, namely the question of whether OC sentences can be interpreted *referentially*.[1] A referential interpretation renders an OC sentence false whenever its singular term fails to refer, and that is surely incorrect. Extensionality, however, requires only that *if* the singular term does refer, then replacing it by another co-designative singular term will not change truth-value. It is not inconceivable, they would claim, that despite the failure of the referential analysis of OC sentences, they are still extensional, i.e., that arguments of the form ‘T is ontologically committed to a & a=b, therefore T is ontologically committed to b’ are valid. Now while in a literal sense their point must be admitted, I think that it contributes nothing to the understanding of OC sentences, nor to semantics in general. Although the possibility they allege can be described without formal contradiction or paradox, we have every reason to believe that it is never realized. For, the only reason we ever have to think that an argument of the form ‘φa & a=b, therefore φb’ is valid is that the ‘a’ and ‘b’ slots require expressions whose sole

[1] Jubien, 1972.

function in the 'ϕ——' context is to name something, and hence since 'a=b' guarantees that they name the same thing, one can be substituted for the other without change of truth-value. The only (apparent) exception in fact serves to prove the rule. It might be argued that ''——' denotes ——' is a context in which terms like 'George' do not function solely referentially (since on its first occurrence it will appear between quotes), and yet substitution of identicals preserves truth-value in this context. The facts must be admitted, but the example fails to drive the kind of wedge between referentiality and extensionality which affects OC sentences. The reason is that in order for ''George' denotes George' to be true, 'George' must denote. Thus even if we were to analyse the role of 'George' in ''George' denotes George' as *more* than referential, it would still be a role which *presumes* that 'George' denotes. Hence this example provides no support to the idea that a context which allows *non*-denoting terms may nevertheless be extensional. And if the interpretation of the example is that, roughly speaking, the effect of the quotes is undone by 'denotes', then we will deny that the role of 'George' in ''George' denotes George' is more than referential, and hence the example drives no wedge at all between referentiality and extensionality.

Although the argument presented above establishes non-extensionality, there are intuitions concerning OC sentences which seem to require referential analysis. In what follows I shall consider the most popular of those intuitions and endeavour to explain how to understand them so as to preserve the non-referentiality of OC sentences.

Some have claimed that the following are true:

(3)　'($\exists$x)(x is a prime number)' is ontologically committed to abstract objects.[2]

(4)　'($\exists$x)(x = the president of the U.S. who resigned in 1974)' is ontologically committed to Richard Nixon.

Their reasoning goes as follows: it is certainly true that

(3a)　'($\exists$x)(x is a prime number)' is ontologically committed to prime numbers

---

[2] Quine, 1961, 103.

and

(4a) '($\exists$x)(x = the president of the U.S. who resigned in 1974)' is ontologically committed to the president of the U.S. who resigned in 1974.

Moreover,

(3b) All prime numbers are abstract objects

and

(4b) The president of the U.S. who resigned in 1974 = Richard Nixon

are true, and it is supposed that (3) follows from (3a) and (3b), and that (4) follows from (4a) and (4b). But the only route that the proposed deductions could follow is to interpret 'prime numbers' in (3a) and the 'president of the U.S. who resigned in 1974' in (4a) referentially, and we have already seen that this is unacceptable. It may be added here that, were we to accept these "deductions", we would be forced to accept the following "deduction" as well:

(5a) '($\exists$x)(x is a unicorn)' is ontologically committed to unicorns

(5b) All unicorns are griffins

(5) (Therefore) '($\exists$x)(x is a unicorn)' is ontologically committed to griffins.

But obviously (5a) and (5b) are true and (5) is false. Thus this form of argument is invalid.

Some have wished to argue, on the contrary, that (3) and (4) are false.[3] Their reasoning (with respect to (4)—the case for (3) is the same) goes as follows: suppose someone were to assert the following theory:

(T) ($\exists$x)(x = the president . . . 1974) & $\sim$($\exists$x)(x = Richard Nixon).

If (4) is right, then T is ontologically committed to Richard Nixon. But, in the light of T's second conjunct, T also explicitly denies Richard Nixon's existence. Thus T is making contradictory commitments, or, more accurately, contradictory pronouncements concerning Richard Nixon's existence. But T is perfectly consistent (though false).

---

[3] Scheffler and Chomsky, 1958–9.

Thus it is incorrect to portray T as making contradictory commitments. And since T certainly is committed to Richard Nixon's non-existence, (4) must be wrong in imputing to T a commitment to his existence.

This argument is mistaken; it turns on a confusion between the contradictoriness of a theory T, and the conflict between the ontological commitment T makes and its explicit pronouncements concerning non-existence. There is no reason to suppose that the latter implies the former. There is no direct route from 'T is ontologically committed to a and T logically implies '$\sim(\exists x)(x = a)$'' to 'T is self-contradictory'. We need at least a bridge in the form of analysis of ontological commitment. If such analysis requires for commitment to a that T logically imply '$(\exists x(x = a)$' then indeed we will reach the conclusion that T is self-contradictory. But this conclusion is not the fruit of intuition, but analysis. Thus it cannot be used against someone who wishes to support the referentiality of OC sentences: he will insist that the conclusion cannot be reached at all, and that those who think it can are merely presupposing their own analysis. His explanation of the failure of T will be that we who know that the president ... 1974 = Richard Nixon also know that T is false, but that T itself is perfectly consistent. It is a consequence of this view that a theory's commitments will often be a matter of contingent fact. Thus one who espouses T may stoutly deny that he is committed to Richard Nixon, though he in fact will be so committed. But the "referentialist" need not be too much troubled by this consequence; the epistemological situation is not very different from one who denies liability with respect to a logical consequence of a theory he holds, being unaware that it is in fact a logical consequence of his theory.

An argument for (4)'s truth and one for its falsity have been rejected; what is the correct view? The correct view is that (4) (and (3) as well) are false. My reason for holding this view is mainly negative: the only reason I can see for allowing (4) to be true is a referential analysis of OC sentences, and that is impossible. Furthermore, I think the intuition that there is something to (4) may be explained by invoking the ontological commitment of a theory relative to an assumption, which may be defined as the commitment of the theory plus the assumption. Obviously, if we add 'The president ... 1974 = Richard Nixon' to '$(\exists x)(x = \text{president} ... 1974)$', we arrive at a theory which is committed to Richard Nixon. And since the addition is a truth known to us all, we pay scant attention to it. If *I* were to hold T then I, given the other things I believe (including the crucial assumption), will be committed to Richard Nixon, but '$(\exists x)(x = $ the president ... 1974)' by itself is not.

Some at this point would wish to revive the distinction between referentiality and extensionality for OC sentences. Referentiality was rejected due to unacceptable consequences for theories with commitments to non-existents. (4), by contrast, concerns substitutivity with respect to theories whose ontological commitments are satisfied. This suggests that we recognize two notions of ontological commitment: one for false theories which indeed will be non-referential, and a referential one for true theories which will permit the kind of consequence which (4) embodies. They may even cite Nelson Goodman's treatment of representation with respect to pictures.[4] If a picture represents some existent, then it denotes that existent, says Goodman. If, however, it is a picture in the representational style which represents no existent, say a picture of Zeus, then the notion of representation is non-referential: the picture is a Zeus-picture, where 'Zeus-picture' is a predicate with which pictures are classified, on a par with 'landscape' and 'surrealist'. With respect to ontological commitment they would suggest that if T is committed to an existent a, then a referential analysis is in order, while if T is committed to a non-existent, then a non-referential analysis is in order.

I reject this line of argument: it is certainly wrong with respect to ontological commitment, and I am inclined to think it is mistaken with respect to pictorial representation as well. I will start with the latter point. If there is a purely monadic, classificatory predicate 'Zeus-picture' (I am convinced that there is), then there surely is also a purely classificatory predicate 'George Washington-picture'. The two predicates are learned much in the same way, and have the same logical force. It may well be that a picture of George Washington, *in addition to being a George Washington-picture*, also denotes George Washington. That is, when a picture represents some existent, we may very well say that the relation it has to that existent is denotation; but that does not deprive the picture of its classificatory status: it is no less a George Washington-picture due to George Washington's existence. Likewise, even if some referential analysis of ontological commitment is reasonable for those theories which are committed to existents, we must have in addition a non-referential analysis which applies to true

---

[4] Goodman, 1976, 21–6.

and false theories alike, and that notion will be non-extensional. This is the result of pursuing the analogy with pictures, if my criticism of Goodman's theory be accepted. But whatever the case is with pictures, there must be one non-referential analysis of ontological commitment which applies to all theories. For, a theory's ontological commitment is one determinant of its truth: if a theory is committed to what does not exist, then it is false. The converse, however, does not hold: whether or not it bears a particular ontological commitment is not determined by whether it is true or false. If, however, there were two notions of ontological commitment, one for true theories and one for false ones, the commitment of a theory would depend upon its truth. If the theory were true, it would have only referential ontological commitment; if false, it would have only non-referential ontological commitment. This would reverse the true order of dependence.

Furthermore, the suggestion of two notions of ontological commitment cannot be made precise without circularity. For it will surely not be suggested that the non-referential interpretation be applied merely because the theory in question is false for some reason or other. For example, if the commitment of '$(\exists x)(x = \text{Zeus})$' to Zeus is to be declared non-referential, this is not due to the *mere falsity* of '$(\exists x)(x = \text{Zeus})$', for then we should have to declare the commitment of '$(\exists x)(x = \text{Richard Nixon}) \, \& \, 2+2=5$' to Richard Nixon non-referential as well.

Rather, the commitment of '$(\exists x)(x = \text{Zeus})$' will be taken as non-referential because its commitment to Zeus is unfulfilled—because if we take the commitment it has to Zeus as referential, the commitment cannot be sustained, and we know that it is committed to Zeus. If this is the manner in which it is to be decided which commitments are referential and which not, clearly we are moving in a circle: first we need to know what the commitment will be to see whether it can sustain a referential interpretation, and then we will decide which interpretation to give it. The prior decision must be made in terms of a notion of ontological commitment which applies to all theories, and hence a non-referential notion. I should add that while I see no problem for a proposed *addition* of a referential notion of ontological commitment for true theories, I see no need for it either. (This is in contrast to the case of pictorial representation where the need is clear.)

There are other intuitions concerning the general nature of ontological commitment which seem to support a referential analysis of OC sentences. Some wish to argue as follows: To say that T is committed to a is to say that in order for T to be true, a must exist. But if a = b, then if a exists, b also exists. Therefore, in order for T to be true, b must exist.[5] This argument is a plain modal fallacy, which becomes obvious the minute the argument is formalized. The crucial point is the ambiguity of the first premiss: one formulation validates the argument but falsifies the premiss, and the other achieves the opposite. Here is the formalization:

(6a) If T, then $(\exists x)$(necessarily $(x = a)$)

(6b) Necessarily (If T, then $(\exists x)(x = a)$)

(7)   a=b

(8a) If T, then $((\exists x)$ necessarily $(x = b))$

(8b) Necessarily (If T, then $(\exists x)(x = b)$).

(6a) and (7) imply (8a), but (6a) is false; (6b) is true, but (6b) and (7) do not imply (8b). When the argument is formalized the fallacy is obvious, but it is often covered up by misleading prose. "If a must exist for T to be true, and a = b how could T be true if b didn't exist?" If we demand large scope for 'must' and 'could', the question becomes: "If necessarily (If T then $(\exists x)(x = a)$) and a = b, how is it that not necessarily (If T then $(\exists x)(x = b)$)?" The answer is then obvious: we cannot substitute co-extensive terms in a modal context and expect truth-value to be preserved. If it is still felt that the question is not being directly answered, perhaps this will help: T *could* still be false even if b did not exist *if it were the case that a ≠ b*. The question assumes that 'a = b' contributes directly to the ontological commitment of T. This is not the case, unless you pass to T' by adding 'a = b' to T; then we do get the conclusion that *T'* is committed to b.

There are those who will not be totally satisfied with this argument. If we are taking the modal paraphrase of ontological commitment seriously—T is committed to a iff necessarily (if T then $(\exists x)(x = a)$) —then of course mere co-extensivity of terms will not allow substitutivity, but necessary coextensivity will. So perhaps (4) is false, but the following are true:

(9)   '$(\exists x)(x = 3+3)$' is ontologically committed to 6

(10) '$(\exists x)(x = Cicero)$' is ontologically committed to Tully.

---

[5] Though I have not found this argument explicitly in print, I have heard it often in conversation.

More generally, the question is this: are we prepared to take the modal paraphrase so seriously that we will regard the following form of argument as valid:

(N) T is ontologically committed to a—i.e. necessarily (If T then $(\exists x(x = a))$
Necessarily $(a = b)$
Therefore, T is ontologically committed to b—i.e. necessarily (If T then $(\exists x)(x = b)$).

Notice that the argument form (N) is valid independently of how 'necessarily' is understood. In order to evaluate (9), (10), and (N), we shall have to probe the modal paraphrase itself. It is often pointed out that the philosopher who initiated the discussion of ontological commitment, W. V. Quine, has repeatedly used modal idioms to express the notion, in spite of his life-long opposition to the use of modality in philosophy.[6] The most likely interpretation of his writings, it seems, is to treat the modal idioms as loose for logical implication.[7] However, whatever Quine's intentions may be, we must address ourselves to the broader question of the applicability of (N) no matter what kind of modality is employed. And this question is a live one for even so narrow a view as Quine's, since some singular terms are demonstrably coextensive (e.g. '(ix)(Fx)' and '(ix)((Fx & Gx) v (Fx & ~Gx))').

What then shall we say about (N)? It is clearly a valid argument form. Thus if we accept any modal paraphrase of ontological commitment we will be forced to acknowledge (N). The only alternative is to reject modality altogether in the expression of ontological commitment; but then our intuitions seem to evaporate altogether. I shall defend a position of minimum use of (N) by accepting only logical necessity. Substitutivity will be licensed only due to demonstrable coextensiveness.

If we leave aside logical necessity, I have two objections to the use of the necessity paraphrase. First, it requires the use of notions which are unclear and philosophically controversial. This is not only a statement of personal bias: it has the justification of economy behind it. If we can adequately analyse ontological commitment without using those notions we may expect to be understood by a much wider range

---

[6] Cartwright, 1954, and Chihara, 1973, 87 ff.
[7] Oliver, 1974.

of philosophers than otherwise (assuming we make use of no other questionable notions). Second, the further down we go on the list of notions of necessity, the harder it becomes to see the result as a paraphrase of the commitments *of T itself*, rather than of T together with some extra assumptions. Consider physical necessity. Let T be '$(\exists x)(x$ = the ball released at time t 64 feet above the earth's surface)'. Is T committed to the ball which hit the earth at time t + 2 seconds? The mere fact that the two balls are the same is irrelevant here: we have rejected full referentiality and extensionality for OC sentences. The question is: does the fact that the balls are necessarily the same—that their identity follows from certain physical laws—allow us to derive the extended commitment? On the one hand it is quite true that T cannot (i.e., it is physically impossible that T) be true unless there exists a ball which hit the ground at t + 2 seconds. On the other hand, that fact is the product of two factors: the commitment of T directly to the ball released etc., and the physically necessary consequences of that commitment. *Given the world as it is*, more precisely, *given the laws of nature*, T cannot be true unless the ball that hit the ground exists. But this is a fact about T and the laws of nature: change either of these factors and the necessity is lost. Thus it is incorrect to call this the ontological commitment of T.

Perhaps an analogy will help clarify the point. Suppose we introduce a general notion of *truth commitment*, i.e., that which must be *true* for a theory T to be true. This will be a relation between theories and sentences. How shall the 'must' be understood? If we speak of a theory's truth commitment as that which, if not satisfied, renders the theory false, then the universal procedure is to construe a theory's commitments as the logical closure of the set of sentences which the theory asserts. In other words, 'must' is understood in terms of logical necessity. But, in the light of the previous paragraph, perhaps we should consider wider notions: e.g., that whose truth follows with physical necessity from the theory. And yet, such notions are unheard of. Why? Because, I suggest, to say that T is physically committed to S is a misleading way of saying that if T is true then the laws of nature require the truth of S, and thus the truth of S is necessitated by two factors—the truth of T and the laws of nature—and so is not strictly speaking a commitment of T at all. The same may be said for ontological commitment. Furthermore, these reflections are applicable as well to all other notions of necessity which are at present under discussion (i.e., all such notions, except logical necessity). In each case, while it may well be true that if T is true then some thing must exist, the connection between T and that thing's existence will be mediated—by the metaphysical structure of the world, by the necessary connections between our concepts, or what have you. In each case the mediation renders it inappropriate to record the necessity as the commitment of T alone.

Now we must turn our attention to logical necessity. What I am claiming is that the following is the only necessity paraphrase which is legitimate:

(*)   T is ontologically committed to a iff it is logically necessary that if T is true then $(\exists x)(x = a)$,

or equivalently:

T is ontologically committed to a iff T logically implies
'$(\exists x)(x = a)$'.

The question is: why does the argument just given not apply to this sense of necessity as well? It is true that we allow logical necessity to determine the truth commitment of a theory. Thus my position is in accord with common practice. But perhaps the question should be put to the common practice. If T does not assert S, but only logically implies S, why do we not regard the relationship between T and S as mediated by logic, and hence not the sole liability of T? Now there is a theory of logic which has a direct answer to this question. This theory holds that logic merely explicates the content of sentences; that the conclusion of a logically valid argument adds no information to the premisses; that logical truths are utterly empty of content. Thus the "mediation" of logic amounts to nothing: that which follows logically from T *is asserted by T*; logic only reveals some of the things which T asserts which are not obvious on the surface. Thus the logical consequences of sentences asserted by T are properly called the commitment of T itself.

But I do not subscribe to this view of logic: I think the contribution of logic is non-trivial, and that is reflected in the fact that logic can be challenged for empirical reasons. This is not the place to debate this issue, but rather to assess its significance for the understanding of ontological commitment. The significance is this: if we accept (*) at all, we do so only by courtesy. Though there are many important differences between the various notions of necessity, they all have this in common: what follows necessarily from what a theory asserts is a non-trivial extension of what the theory asserts. Thus it would indeed make sense to hold T committed only to those sentences which it explicitly asserts, and to count the commitment to their logical consequences as the product of two factors—the truth of T and logic. But as a matter of fact, logic is so well entrenched that in most contexts the logical consequences of a theory's explicitly asserted sentences *are treated as if* the theory asserted them directly. Ordinarily, if one of its logical consequences is refuted, the theory is immediately regarded as refuted, even though this is not the only possible outcome of such a confrontation. It is out of courtesy to this treatment of theories that we accept (*), if we accept it all; and I propose to accept it for that reason.

The result is that the argument form (N) receives the narrowest possible application: substitutivity in the context 'T is ontologically committed to ——' is allowed only due to logically necessary coextensiveness of terms. Thus (9) will be rejected: if it is not a truth of logic that $3 + 3 = 6$. On the other hand, (10) raises special problems. What kind of necessity is appropriate to 'Cicero = Tully'? Some think it is logical necessity, and hence will support (10).[8] They argue that what 'Cicero = Tully' asserts is no more than the self-identity of Cicero, and surely that is logically necessary. I disagree; I take seriously the formality of logic, and hence do not regard '$a = b$' and '$a = a$' on a par, even if 'a' and 'b' are replaced with rigid designators. Again, I cannot argue this here; suffice it to say that once (*) is accepted, the range of substitutivity allowed in OC sentences will be affected by one's views on this question.

There are those who feel that if (*) is all there is to ontological commitment then the whole concept is trivial.[9] In a sense this is true, but in that sense it was meant to be trivial, and hence this shows the success of (*).[10] What was the notion of ontological commitment expected to accomplish? It was supposed to tell us *at what points our language links up with the world of objects*. The problem was that some philosophers were too naïve about how the link is accomplished. They espoused doctrines such as: every singular term (where the notion of singular term is given a rough grammatical criterion, e.g., 'proper name or paraphrasable into the form 'the such-and-such'') names some thing in each sentence in which it occurs. When confronted with singular terms like 'Mr Pickwick' and 'The king of the

---

[8] Kripke, 1972.
[9] Scheffler and Chomsky, 1958–9.
[10] Quine, 1968 [41], 91–9.

U.S.' which at first blush do not name anything, they invented entities for the singular terms to name and paraphrased the sentences in which they occur so as to fit the semantical facts. Russell responded with the theory of descriptions which, due to a different interpretation of the semantical contribution of singular terms to the sentences in which they occur, enabled those sentences to have a determinate truth-value even when they named nothing. But for simple sentences it remained the case that if the singular term does not name anything the sentence cannot be *true*. But, as Quine observed, there are many simple sentences which are true and yet which contain singular terms which do not name—or at least which we do not wish to regard as naming anything.[11] A few examples are: 'Honesty is rare', 'The dog is an animal', 'He did it for the sake of peace', and 'The average American earns $10,000 a year.' The point is that no simple grammatical description of the class of "singular terms" will be able to pick out those which we use to name objects and those which we do not. How then shall they be distinguished? In a sentence 'Fa' the 'a' is used to name something just in case we are prepared to infer '$(\exists x)Fx$'—this is the answer Quine gave. What does this answer tell us? Two things: (a) the quantifiers are *always* used to refer to the world of objects, and (b) whether or not a seeming singular term is so used can be discovered on the basis of its relationship to the quantifiers. Thus our language links up with the world of objects via its quantifiers, and the rest of language participates in the link in so far as it is properly related to the quantifiers. We shall have reason to question this doctrine below, especially part (a), but for the time being it must be emphasized what the notion of ontological commitment was *not* designed to accomplish. It was not intended as a theory or explication of the mechanism of reference. It was not intended to answer the age-old riddle of how the world and language interact so as to produce truth and falsity, except in so far as it helps identify the points of contact. It may be due to overestimating the significance of the question to which Quine addressed himself that some have felt that his answer is over-trivial. I think their charge is entirely mistaken: Quine's answer is quite *appropriate* to the question he asked, even though I think it is not quite *true*, as we shall see in chapter III.

Another objection which may be raised against (*) is that it restricts ontological commitment to languages which have singular terms.

[11] Quine, 1939.

then IITs do not represent the real semantic characteristics of the theories we espouse and which are the media of our commitments. Part of my difference with Jubien lies in the gap I discern between my FLA's and his IIT's.

The following is one of Jubien's examples of an IIT. The schemata comprising T are

$$(\exists x)(\exists y)(x \neq y) \ (\exists x)(y)(Rxy \ \& \ (z)(\exists w)(Rzw \supset z=x)).$$

The int. int. I provides $\{a,b,c\}$ as T's domain and $\{(a,a),(a,b),(a,c),(b,b),(b,c)\}$ as the extension of 'R' in every world in which T is true. Jubien's intuition concerning (T,I) is that it is committed to the existence of a and nothing else, and this gives rise to two problems in formulating his criterion. The first is that the IIT should not be committed to objects which happen to exist in all worlds, and yet are not in any way mentioned in the IIT. So we cannot say that an IIT is committed to each thing which exists in every world in which the IIT is true; that will let in all necessary existents, for example. The problem is solved roughly by allowing commitment only when the object is in the domain of all *submodels* of the IIT, even if some of those submodels are not values of the int. int. function for any possible world. Thus if * is a necessary existent, (T,I) escapes commitment to * because even though * exists in every *world* in which (T,I) is true, there is a submodel of (T,I) in that world in which T is true—namely, the restriction of (T,I) to the domain of that world minus *. And this would be true even if I were to give $\{a,b,c,*\}$ as T's domain in all worlds in which T is true, since the submodel need not be a value of I.

The second problem is that an IIT in which we have a theorem of the form '$(\exists x)(y)(Fy \equiv y=x)$' and whose int. int. provides that 'Fx' be satisfied by the same (possible) entity in all models which are values of the int. int., should, according to Jubien, be committed to that object. But there may be submodels which are not values of the int. int. from whose domains that object is missing. The solution is to expand all the submodels considered in solving the first problem by adding in all objects which meet the above description. If we call them the *expanded submodels*, then a rough formulation of Jubien's criterion is the following:

(J)   An IIT (T,I) is ontologically committed to a (possible) entity a iff a is a member of every expanded submodel of every model provided for T by I.

For the example (T,I), commitment is wanted with respect to a. However, there is a submodel of (T,I) in which T is true and in which a does not exist, e.g. take {b,c} as the domain and {(b,b),(b,c)} as the extension of 'R'. Here the role of "least R" is played by b instead of a. Nevertheless, since the int. int. which "gives the meaning" of the predicate letter 'R' decrees that a be the "least R", the suggested submodel is felt to be untrue to the intended content of (T,I) and hence unjustly deprives (T,I) of its commitment to a. (J) solves this problem by considering only the *expanded* submodels of (T,I). An expanded submodel must contain every entity whose unique existence can be proved in T; thus no submodel excluding a is relevant to the commitments of (T,I). (J) thus commits (T,I) to a in accord with Jubien's intuitions.

Here are some consequences of (J). (1) An ITT can be committed to a particular even though it contains no singular term referring to that particular, as is the case for (T,I). (2) An IIT can be committed to a particular even if it contains no theorem of the form '$(\exists x)(y)(Fy \equiv y=x)$'. For, it may contain a predicate P such that $\ulcorner(\exists x)Px\urcorner$ is a theorem and the int. int. provides that P receive the same singleton as extension in all submodels of all the int. int.'s models. The member of that singleton will be a member of every submodel of every model provided by the int. int.

To complete the exposition of Jubien's theory, I will record his strong insistence on the use of logical possibility in interpreting ontological commitment. He writes:

To achieve a precise definition we turn to a very broad notion of *logical possibility* – one in which for any situation consistently describable in the language of the theory, there would be a world in which that situation held. This notion is presumably broader than that of *real* (or *metaphysical*) possibility. Thus, though it may be metaphysically impossible that Cicero $\neq$ Tully, there is a logically possible world in which this holds.[13]

I applaud this decision, though we shall have to se to what extent Jubien maintains it consistently.

Consequences (1) and (2) illustrate the difference between Jubien's theory and mine. For me (in contrast to (1)) a FLA cannot be committed to a unless 'a' appears in its vocabulary. And since this will automatically produce the theorem '$(\exists x)(y)(y=a \equiv y=x)$', I reject (2)

[13] Jubien, 1974, 524.

as well. In other words, for me *an FLA is committed to a only if it contains or logically implies a sentence whose form determines that it makes that commitment*; for Jubien the commitment may be due to the semantics in so large a measure that from the syntax alone we would never suspect it at all.

This contrast deserves clarification through an example. However, this is not easy to do. For, (J) applies to IIT's, while my criterion applies to FLA's. To give an example to which the contrasting views apply we need a FLA and an IIT which do not differ in relevant respects, and this appears to beg the question of the adequacy of possible worlds semantics. Nevertheless let us try. Consider again the example (T,I). (T,I) is committed to a even though it has no name for a, since it has '$(\exists x)(y)((z)(Rzy \supset z=y) \equiv y=x)$' as a theorem and I provides that a is the only thing satisfying '$(y)((z)(Rzy \supset z=y) \equiv y=x)$' in each of the domains of the worlds in which I makes T true. Now we need to find an FLA F which will correspond closely enough to (T,I) so that the application of my criterion to F will provide a *contrast* to Jubien's treatment of (T,I)—a contrast, that is, and not merely a change of subject. We need two predicates, one to provide the range of the quantifiers, and one in place of 'R', which seem to have the semantics described by I.

One way to do this is to make use of rigid designators for the objects a, b, and c, say 'A', 'B', and 'C'. The two predicates then are '$x=A \lor x=B \lor x=C$' (to fix the domain) and '$(x=A \& y=A) \lor (x=A \& y=B) \lor (x=A \& y=C) \lor (x=B \& y=B) \lor (x=B \& y=C)$'. But then we will have individual constants in the language of T itself, and then Jubien and I would agree that T is committed to each of a, b, and c. We might think of mathematical predicates, but Jubien explicitly declares his criterion (J) irrelevant to abstracta.

We might think of a predicate which expresses an essential property of the objects which satisfy it, but this will not do the job unless we have very strong assumptions about the relations between the universes of existents in the possible worlds. For example, perhaps 'made of wood' is essential to the things which have it, but in different possible worlds, different things are made of wood.

We might try relaxing the requirement on the needed predicates in accordance with (J): they need to have the desired extensions only in those worlds in which I makes T true. Now T says that there are at least two things, having a certain characteristic (fixing the domain), and exactly one thing having that characteristic which bears R to all the rest. For any possible world H, I does one of two things: either (i) I makes T true in H by providing at least two things in the domain of quantification and giving R an extension such that only one thing in the domain bears R to all the rest—and in fact it does this by taking {a,b,c} as the domain of quantification and {(a,a),(a,b),(a,c),(b,b),(b,c)} as the extension of R; or (ii) I makes T false in H either by not providing two things for the domain of quantification or by giving R an extension such that it is not the case that a unique member of the domain bears R to all the rest. We are looking for predicates which will have the required extensions in all the worlds in groups (i) and appropriate extensions in the worlds in group (ii). Now since *all* we know about I from Jubien's example is that it divides all possible worlds between (i) and (ii), and since there are many different ways of doing this, we need to specify I more completely before we can search for the desired predicates. For example, we could put the real world in group (i) and all others in group (ii), or we could reverse the choices, and we would obviously need two different pairs of predicates to reflect the difference. For the sake of finding a contrast between Jubien's approach and mine, it would suffice to find one such specification of I for which an appropriate pair of predicates can be found. (From this point of view, we may understand the previous paragraph as an argument that the specification which puts all possible worlds in group (i) creates an I for which the needed predicates do not exist.) Or, putting the require-ments in the opposite order, we need to find two predicates which have the requisite extensions in one group of possible worlds (which we may then take as the worlds of group (i) in our specification of I), and whose extensions in all other possible worlds may be anything at all so long as they falsify T (so that those worlds can form group (ii)).

To appreciate how difficult it will be to do this, consider one half of the requirement. Taking into consideration only the domain predicate, what we would need is a predicate P whose extension in some possible worlds is precisely {a,b,c} and whose extension in all other possible worlds has one member or none. How is this possible? P is satisfied by only a, b, and c in a world H, and (a) it is impossible—*logically* impossible—to "alter" H such that (i.e., it is logically impossible that there be a world H′ just like H except that) something else in addition to a, b, and c satisfies P, or something else in place of one of them satisfies P, or exactly one of them does not satisfy P; and yet (b) there may be worlds in which one thing different from a, b, and c satisfies P!

To make the (a) half work we naturally think of a predicate P essential to a, b, and c and whose negation is essential to everything else but then the (b) part requires that in some possible worlds something other than a, b, and c satisfy P, hence we have a contradiction. And even (a) by itself is in trouble: it may be easy to find predicates which are essential to the things which satisfy them and whose negations are essential to everything else, but it is much harder to find one which *in addition* essentially characterizes a *particular trio* (since there are supposed to be no possible worlds in which only two of a, b, and c exist and satisfy P). Obviously run-of-the-mill essentials like 'human' and 'made of wood' won't do. The most likely candidate is rather controversial: genesis predicates like 'child of John and Mary' or 'developed from zygote Z'. There is disagreement as to whether such predicates are really essential of their bearers, but let's suppose they are. But how shall we introduce the trio commitment? It might be thought that 'is one of the three children of John and Mary will do', i.e., '$(\exists x)(\exists y)(\exists z)(x,y,z$ are children of John and Mary & $x{\neq}y$ & $y{\neq}z$ & $x{\neq}z$ & $(w)(w$ is a child of John and Mary $\supset (w{=}x \lor w{=}y \lor w{=}z)))$'. But while this carries a commitment to John and Mary parenting exactly three children, it does not specify *who* those children are. Thus this predicate will have a three-membered extension in all possible worlds where it is non-empty, but those extensions may have very different members. The problem is to get a commitment to a *specific* trio, without introducing names for its members (otherwise we have lost the contrast we sought, as we saw above). Even the appeal to zygotes will not help. Imagine that a, b, and c are people who developed from zygotes Z, Z', and Z'' respectively. We try to characterize the domain via the predicate 'x developed from one of Z, Z', Z''). We may assume that developing from a particular zygote is essential to its bearer; thus in every world in which a exists, a develops from Z. We may assume further that it is essential to a zygote that it not develop into anything else; thus in every world in which Z develops, it develops into a. But there are worlds in which Z is aborted in the first week of pregnancy. If, in such a world, Z' and Z'' do develop into b and c, we will fail the requirement that in no world do exactly two of a, b, and c satisfy the domain predicate.

Although these considerations do not amount to a proof, I think it is clear that it is very unlikely that this IIT represents the semantics of any pair of predicates in a functioning language. This makes me suspect that IITs are not really theories at all, and that (J) is plausible, if at all, only for those artificially concocted IITs which have no bearing on real life.

Let's try again, this time with consequence (2). We want an IIT which is committed to a even though it contains no unique existence theorems. Let T' have '$(\exists x)Px$' as its non-logical axiom, and let I' provide that in all possible worlds the domain of the interpretation is the set of physical objects existing in that world, and that the extension of 'P' in all worlds where a exists is $\{a\}$ where a is some physical object, and empty in all other worlds. (J) says that (T',I') is committed to a. Our problem is to find the domain predicate and predicate for 'P'. For the domain predicate we may choose 'is a physical object'. And for 'P' it seems that we can choose a predicate expressing an "individual essence", i.e., a property which is essential to exactly one thing. Following Quine, let's take 'is-Socrates' and abbreviate it 'Sx'. (T',I') says that something is-Socrates. It is committed to the particular Socrates by (J) because, unlike IIT's which say that something is green, or that something is wooden, (T',I') says that something meets a condition that *only one thing could meet*, and that thing is Socrates. In this example the heavy burden borne by the semantics is especially striking: there is no hint from the form of the axiom '$(\exists x)Sx$' that commitment to a particular is in the offing.

I would acquiesce in this example, but for one thing: I don't think it is true that 'Sx' expresses a condition that only one thing *can* meet, if we understand 'can' in terms of logical possibility as Jubien suggests (and with which I agree). For, the concept of logical possibility provides that every situation consistently describable in the language of T' is true in some possible world. Thus there is a possible world H in which '$(\exists x)(\exists y)(x \neq y \ \& \ Sx \ \& \ Sy)$' is true, and so it is not true that 'Sx' has the same extension in all possible worlds (nor does it have the same extension in all worlds in which T' is true—obviously, adding elements to the extension of 'Sx' will not make T false). Now the extension of 'Sx' in H has at least two members, Socrates and something else (call it Plato). Thus I' cannot be as we supposed in the last paragraph: it cannot assign the singleton $\{Socrates\}$ as the extension of 'Sx' is every possible world. Furthermore, by (J) we no longer have commitment to Socrates, since by restricting the domain and the extension of 'Sx' to $\{Plato\}$ we obtain a submodel of (T',I') in H in which T is true and in which Socrates does not exist. Thus a consistent commitment to Jubien's very broad notion of logical possibility deprives us of (at least this case of) commitment to particulars by theories without unique existence theorems.

Apart from the failure of Jubien's claim of ontological commitment without uniqueness theorems, there is a more general moral to be learned from the impossibility of the intensional interpretation I'. Even if we agree to represent the intensions of predicates as functions from possible worlds to extensions, it does not follow that we have provided the intension of a predicate whenever we have provided such a function. This mode of representation of intensions is essentially richer than the linguistic setting to which it is applied: there are functions from possible worlds to classes of possible entities which do not represent the intension of any predicate. In particular, any function which is constant and whose value is a singleton will not represent the intension of a predicate.

Now you may ask: apparently it has been shown that 'is-Socrates' is not necessarily true of Socrates. Does this mean that no non-tautological predicate is necessarily true of any thing? And if so, then no such predicate holds essentially of any thing?! The answer is that it has *not* been shown that 'is-Socrates' *does not express an individual essence*. To think otherwise is to confuse *metaphysical* and *logical* necessity (which Jubien keeps admirably distinct). To express an essence is to be a predicate satisfied by one and the same thing in all *metaphysically* possible worlds (in which that thing exists), since what properties are essences is a matter of *metaphysical*, and not *logical* necessity. But ontological commitment is a matter of logical necessity, and hence we must take into account all logically possible worlds in which our commitments are met. The situation is exactly parallel to the example of Cicero which Jubien gives. For Jubien (and I agree), '$(\exists x)(x = \text{Cicero})$' is not committed to Tully, even though 'Cicero' and 'Tully' are rigid designators, since their rigidity is a matter of metaphysics, and not of logic. And his remark concerning rigidity forestalls a natural response to the objection to 'is-Socrates', namely that that predicate is understood in terms of the name 'Socrates'—it has its extension fixed via the name—and hence has a unique extension in all possible worlds. This response presumes that rigid designators have *logical* power to fix the extension of a predicate, and this is not the case. Or at least we may say that Jubien and I agree that it is not the case, and that is sufficient for the purposes of contrasting our theories. Thus we are again left without an example of a FLA to parallel the IIT which has the commitment in violation of my criterion.

So far, our inability to illustrate the contrast between (J) and my criterion has been due to the fact that for the IIT's to which (J) applies we have found no corresponding FLA's. Perhaps we should reverse the order: start with an FLA and find a corresponding IIT. But recall that we want an FLA–IIT pair which will illustrate the contrast, and that means that the IIT will have a commitment which the FLA lacks. ((J) is uniformly more liberal than my criterion in apportioning commitment, if we conceive of my criterion as being applied to theories which talk about possible objects.) Any such FLA will have no singular term referring to the object in question, and so Jubien will have to acquire the commitment to that object via the int. int. as described above, and then we will have the same question again: is the int. int. a reasonable account of the semantics of the terms of the FLA? So our conclusion seems to be this: (J) differs from my criterion only with respect to IIT's to which no FLA's correspond, and hence Jubien has no critique of my criterion as applied to FLA's. If we agree that FLA's are the real medium of ontological commitment—indeed, the real medium of describing and coming to know about the world—then we must conclude that (J) is altogether superfluous.

Finally, let's assess the situation which results from adding abstract objects—mathematical objects, in particular—to the field of application of (J). (Jubien does not do this for reasons which I shall discuss shortly.) According to custom, the predicate 'natural number having no predecessor' (abbreviated 'Z') is thought of as meeting the above requirement: if we have 'is a natural number' as the domain predicate, then it is usually held that 'Z' has the extension $\{0\}$ in every possible world. But I think this is a mistake. I take my stand with (one part of) Jubien('s words): any consistently describable situation is logically possible. Since '$(\exists x)(\exists y)(Zx \ \& \ Zy \ \& \ x \neq y)$' is consistent, there must be a possible world in which there are two zeros; since '$\sim(\exists x)Zx$' is consistent, there must be a logically possible world in which there is no zero. To think otherwise is again to confuse logical possibility with metaphysical necessity, and it is only the former which is at issue here. Surely there is no inconsistency (however loosely that notion be construed) in the notion of a numberless universe, or a universe in which there are two different things which are used as the starting-points of the otherwise uniform number sequence. In fact, there is no difficulty whatever in imagining such universes. If we pass to consistent sentences such as '$(\exists x)(2 + x = 1)$' imagination begins to fail, but there is no reason to leap to logical failure as the explanation, just as there is no reason to cite logic in explaining why this wooden table could not be (have been?) made of ice, or why nothing other than Socrates could satisfy 'is-Socrates'. Our imagination may be as bound by our metaphysics as by our logic.

It might be suggested that all I have done is to come down hard on Jubien's very broad characterization of logical possibility and use it to trivialize his project: if anything consistently describable is logically possible, and the standard of consistency in description is the first-order calculus, then of course the criterion of ontological commitment will be deducibility of explicit existence assertions! To this charge I plead guilty: my objection to Jubien is that there is an inconsistency between his conception of logical possibility and (J), and that we should choose to keep the former and drop the latter.

I will close this chapter with reactions to some of Jubien's remarks concerning ontological commitment to abstracta. He describes a "paradox" which he calls "the problem of isomorphic inter-pretations". He asks us to consider a theory T of arithmetic with no constants with the property that any final segment of the natural numbers could serve as the domain of an interpretation isomorphic to the standard one. Since 'theory' for Jubien means 'uninterpreted first-order formal system', we may imagine its primitive vocabulary to consist of a monadic predicate-letter (for 'is (a) zero'), a dyadic predicate-letter (for successor), and two triadic predicate-letters (for addition and multiplication), plus first-order syntax. Since this is a completely uninterpreted formal system, any infinite progression will serve as the domain of an interpretation isomorphic to the standard one. Now let S be the standard interpretation, and S* be an isomorphic interpretation with domain $\{1,2,3,\ldots\}$. Concerning the two IIT's (T,S) and (T.S*), Jubien makes the following assertions: (i) we have the intuition that (T,S) is committed to exactly $0,1,2,\ldots$ and that (T,S*) is committed to exactly $1,2,3,\ldots$, and so we seem to feel that (T,S) and (T,S*) have different commitments; (ii) we have the intuition that (T,S) and (T,S*) are identical in content—that anything asserted in the one is asserted "if somewhat obscurely" in order; (iii) we have the intuition that theories which are identical in content ought to have the same commitments (and so we have already reached a contra-diction in our intuitions); (iv) this problem relates essentially to abstract objects whose properties are wholly structural—i.e., consist-ing of relations holding among the abstract objects themselves, as is the case with what arithmetic says about numbers; and (v) a resolution of this problem will require the adoption of a criterion of ontological commitment which is either platonistic in the sense that such structural theories are committed to particular objects, or nominalistic if they are not, and in any case a "philosophically neutral" criterion is not possible. Now (v), if true, is a fact of some importance, and so it is important to see whether Jubien's argument for it can stand.

I agree with (i) but not with (ii). I do not see that whatever we express in (T,S*) we can also express in (T,S) (though the converse is correct). Consider how S* operates. Suppose the monadic predicate-letter of T with the intended interpretation 'is (a) zero' is 'Z' and the letter for successor is 'S'. While their extensions respectively in S are $\{0\}$ and $\{(0,1),(1,2),\ldots\}$, their respective extensions in S* are $\{1\}$ and $\{(1,2),(2,3),\ldots\}$. The differences between the extensions dictate different interpretations for the schemata of T. For example, '$(\exists x)(Zx$ & $(y) \sim Syx)$' says 'zero has no predecessor' in (S,T), but it says '1 has no predecessor' in (T,S*). And that leads to the question: how would we say that zero has no predecessor in (T,S*)? Since S* does not have zero in its domain, it is hard to see how this could be accomplished. One might try the schema '$(\exists x)((\exists y)(Zy$ & $Sxy)$ & $(y) \sim Syx)$', (roughly: something is the predecessor of 1 and it has no predecessors), but this schema is false in S* since nothing in the domain satisfies '$(\exists y)(Zy$ & $Sxy)$' and so it is hard to see the schema as asserting that *zero* has no predecessors: it says that something meeting a condition has no predecessors, but nothing meets the condition. There is no more reason to interpret it as saying that zero has no predecessors than saying that the moon has no predecessors. Thus (ii) is incorrect, and thus the "paradox" consisting of the inconsistent trio (i)–(iii) disappears.

Now let's consider (iv) and (v). What is peculiar about a theory such as arithmetic which describes only how its objects relate to one another, giving only "structural properties" of the elements of its domain? (Note that a number of deep questions lurk here. Does the monadic predicate 'is (a) zero' express a "structural property" of numbers? Similarly, in set theory, does 'has no elements', which picks out the empty set, express a *relation internal* to the field of sets? And does the notion of a theory which describes the entities of which it speaks only in terms of relations to other such entities apply only to theories of abstract objects? In what way are our physical object predicates "non-structural?") On my view there is nothing whatever peculiar about the ontological commitments of such a theory. Arithmetic, for example, as ordinarily interpreted is committed to $0,1,2,\ldots$. Now it is a fact that if we take all the information which arithmetic gives us concerning $0,1,2,\ldots$, there are many questions which are left open concerning their nature, how they relate to other things, and so on. Furthermore, by analysing their place in our overall theory of the world, we may see how to dispense with arithmetic altogether and make do with a substitute, say some portion of set theory. But none of this jeopardizes the ontological commitment of ordinary arithmetic. If there is any problem here at all, it is one of vagueness, or underspecification. But this problem has nothing to do with the contrast between abstract and concrete objects. Imagine a theory of quarks which says merely that they are the constituents of (what are today called) elementary particles. Imagine further that two independent theories of the structure of electrons, et al., are propounded. Which is the theory of the quarks? Neither, yet, unless some decision is made to add a new sentence to the theory saying which is which. The same may be true of arithmetic. There are many progressions which could serve as the numbers (though 1,2, . . . is not one of them—at least, not as handled above). From the axioms of arithmetic alone we cannot decide which is the progression of the numbers, and until some explicit decision is made, we will not be able to decide. But this problem of underspecification has nothing to do with the criterion of commitment and its "philosophical neutrality".

As a consequence of rejecting Jubien's "paradox", I am unwilling to follow him in according to theories which describe only the structural properites of their objects (assuming for the sake of argument that such a class of theories can be isolated, of which I am very sceptical) a special sense of ontological commitment. In effect, what Jubien does is attribute to them commitment to *kinds* of objects, in the following sense: they are committed to the existence of objects which together satisfy their axioms, but have no commitment to which particular objects do this. Thus number theory is committed to the existence of a progression of entities organized so as to satisfy the axioms of number theory, but is not committed to any particular objects as being the elements of the progression. Now I argued above that the mere fact that number theory alone, and perhaps even with the rest of what we know thrown in, does not suffice to determine which entity of my world is the number three, is not a sufficient reason to change our concept of ontological commitment. But if there is a desire to see number theory *not* as committed to particular objects which are underspecified, but as possessing the kind of rarefied commitment Jubien suggests, surely the way to accomplish this is *not* to alter the concept of commitment (which strongly resembles theft), but rather to reformulate the semantics of number theory (honest toil). Of course, if the theory is understood differently, it will have different commit-ments. And this, I suggest, is the correct way to understand what Jubien has actually done. He himself says that he wants to take the theories in question *as asserting* that a certain structure could be exemplified, and that we should treat the constants of such a theory as non-rigid or as predicates which are true of just one thing within any specific domain. No one can quarrel with this procedure: if number theory is understood as having no singular terms, and as having hidden modals so that each assertion is an assertion of possibility, then of course there will be no commitment to the existence of entities which are the numbers in the real world; and this conclusion is drawn on the basis of the one, universal notion of ontological commitment which is indeed philosophically neutral.

The Criterion of Ontological Commitment

In the previous chapter, we saw that OC sentences are neither referential nor extensional, and that the most defensible criterion of ontological commitment is the minimal one:

(*)   T is ontologically committed to a/F's iff T logically implies '$(\exists x)(x = a)$'/'$(\exists x)Fx$'.

The point of the criterion is to enable us to tell which of our expressions refer to objects by helping us resolve context dependence and idiomatic usage. But the quantifiers can effect this resolution only if they are not subject to the same variation of usage as the expressions whose status they are meant to clarify. In fact, quantifiers fail this condition: they are ambiguous between objectual and substitutional usages. When they are used substitutionally, they cannot play their role as referential telltales, and hence (*) is incorrect: it needs to be restricted to the use of objectual quantifiers on the right side. This chapter describes the use of (*) in settling ontological disputes, and in particular the impact of the needed restriction of (*) upon that use.

Let's start with the proposed use of (*) in ontology. The following form of argument is obviously valid:

(A)   T is true.
       T is ontologically committed to a/F's.
       Therefore, a/F's exist(s).

However, whether or not arguments of this form can help us make progress in ontology depends upon our ability to establish the premisses without a fullblooded confrontation with the standard repertoire of metaphysical arguments. Quine contends that this can be done, and the use of (*) to explicate the second premiss of (A)-type arguments is crucial to his claim. For in some cases it appears that a theory T can be established as true prior to determining precisely what its ontological commitments are. If those commitments are wholly a matter of logic, we can discover them without doing ontology directly, and then T's truth may settle outstanding ontological problems. A couple of examples will help clarify this procedure.

Let S be the sentence 'there are exactly as many boys as there are girls'. We may imagine it being verified by a pairing process. At first glance it seems that S may be committed only to boys and girls. Surely there is no other thing whose existence is obviously established by the pairing procedure and which could be counted among S's commitments. Now, however, consider S's logical relations to other sentences. For example, S is usually thought to imply each of the following:

(1) If there are exactly 32 boys, then there are exactly 32 girls.
(2) If there are exactly as many girls as there are symphonies, then there are exactly as many boys as there are symphonies.

The business of logic is to explain these implications by showing them to be instances of valid forms of argument. In many cases this requires restructuring sentences "so as to reveal their logical form" as we say. The accepted method is to analyse them as follows:

(S) The number of boys = the number of girls.
(1) If the number of boys = 32, then the number of girls = 32.
(2) If the number of girls = the number of symphonies, then the number of boys = the number of symphonies.

This makes the implications in question trivialities of the logic of identity. But it also gives us

(3) $(\exists x)(x = $ the number of boys$)$

as a logical consequence of S; and hence commitment to numbers (at least relative to our common assumption that the number of boys is a number). Thus from S's truth, established by pairing, and considerations of logic, we may conclude via an argument of form (A) that there are numbers.

Now let S be the sentence 'the number of apples on the desk = 45' and consider

(4) All Jones's apples and no others are on the desk.

S and (4) together logically imply

(5)   The number of apples belonging to Jones = 45.

But there is nothing in their present form which accounts for the implication. The accepted analysis is this:

(S)   The number of {x: x is an apple on the desk} = 45.
(4)   {x: x is an apple on the desk} = {x: x is an apple belonging to
      Jones}.
(5)   The number of {x: x is an apple belonging to Jones} = 45.

Once it is explained that the context 'the number of ——' is being
understood functionally, identity theory again accounts for the implication. But now (S) implies

(6)   (∃y)(the number of y = 45),

and so S is committed to sets. Now we may imagine S being verified
by a counting procedure, and as before the commitment is established
on the basis of purely logical considerations, thus the conclusion that
there are sets reached via the form (A) argument seems to mark
genuine progress.

Finally, let S be the sentence 'John ran quickly'. If we consult our
untutored logical intuitions, it seems that S logically implies

(7)   John ran.

Nevertheless, if we stick to first order syntax and semantics, the only
known method of showing the implication requires the following
violent restructuring:

(S)   (∃e)(e is by John & e is a running & e is quick).
(7)   (∃e)(e is by John & e is a running).[1]

Here sentences containing predicates describing John are paraphrased by sentences containing predicates which describe what John
did—i.e., an event. Now S may be discovered to be true by a simple
observation, and S is committed to runnings, and thus (relative to the
obviously appropriate assumption that runnings are events) to events.
Here again we discern ontological progress, since the observation of
John running and the analysis of logical form seem to require no direct
appeal to ontology.

It should now be clear how arguments of the form (A) enable (*) to
be used *progressively*, i.e., to establish the existence of (particular or

---

[1] Davidson, 1967 [7].

kinds of) entities without explicit ontological argument. The key to the progressive use of the criterion is our ability to establish the truth of the first premiss of the type (A) argument without fixing T's commitments first and directly inspecting the world to see if the commitment is met.

There are other applications of the criterion which lack this feature—i.e., the truth of T is not established independently of assessing the correctness of its ontological commitment—and hence do not employ type (A) arguments. These are the *conservative* uses of the criterion, as illustrated by the case of particle physics. There is no question of deciding whether a particular theory of electrons, *et al.*, is true before we find out whether or not there are electrons. In fact, the evidence that we have for these theories is a function of their ontological commitments: it is because they are committed to these particles with these specific properties that they can help us explain and predict various phenomena, and those explanations and predictions provide indispensable evidence of their truth. Or consider an astronomical theory which postulates black holes in order to explain certain phenomena: the support for such a theory lies precisely in the fact that the entities to which it is committed have a theoretical impact which is itself evidence for their existence. The conservative use of (*) is characterized by the following type of argument:

(B) T is ontologically committed to a/F's.
The postulation of a/F's is theoretically successful.
Therefore, we have evidence that a/F's exist(s) and that T is true.

Obviously, (B) type arguments are not going to provide striking progress in ontology. They require arguing the case of each new entity explicitly on its scientific/metaphysical merits, with semantics aiding only in determining which theories contribute towards the discussion of which entities.

The progressive use of (*) is clearly the more interesting use from the point of view of philosophy, but its very strength renders it questionable in a way which does not apply to the conservative use. In the examples we saw that from the truth of sentences stating quite common matters of fact, together with purely logical considerations, we could arrive at deep ontological conclusions. Pairing plus logic gave us numbers; counting plus logic gave us classes; observation plus logic gave us events. If we analyse the evidential basis for the premisses of the type (A) arguments used, it appears quite amazing that we can reach such conclusions. The first premiss in each case is established via observation of common physical transactions. The second premiss is established, so it appears, by purely intra-linguistic considerations. Logical implication is a matter of formal truth-preservation: it can be defined and calculated without imputing particular ontological commitments to particular sentences.[2] And from this evidential base we are able to decide that platonism is right and nominalism wrong (since numbers and classes exist), that events exist, and so on. How is this possible?

It may be protested that I am overplaying the strength of the examples: the conclusions only follow if the standard analysis of logical form is the only analysis which will work. If there is another paraphrase of the sentences which accounts for their implications equally well and avoids the commitment, we have no route to the startling conclusions. This qualification of the progressive use of (*) is correct. It is built into type (A) arguments when the second premiss requires that T logically imply '$(\exists x)(x = a)$'/'$(\exists x)Fx$'; a different analysis of logical form will avoid commitment if it can avoid this implication. But even with the understanding that the evidence must include the claim that the proposed logical analysis is the only acceptable analysis, it is startling to reach the ontological conclusions because we are still proceeding solely from bare observation plus intra-linguistic considerations.

When describing why it is that we must countenance numbers and/or classes, Quine often stresses the analogy between those abstract objects and the theoretical objects of physics.[3] Our evidence for both is "indirect", he says, but none the less bona fide evidence for being so. They play an indispensable role in our overall theory of the world, and this is the best evidence we can have for anything. But there appears to be a disanalogy in so far as the objection of the paragraph before last applies to progressive and not to conservative uses of (*). Physics is an instance of the conservative use of (*): the evidence for particles is indeed indirect, *based upon the improvement which accrues to our physical theory from positing their existence.* But we do not use (*) in proving that there are numbers in a parallel fashion: we do not weigh the benefits of positing numbers to our theory of boys,

---

[2] This is the standard approach to logic; for the outline of a nominalist alternative, cf. chapter VI, section (3).

[3] Quine, 1960, 17–25, 266–70.

girls, and pairing, or of positing events to our theory of John and his speed. Indeed, no benefits at all seem to accrue from positing the new entities. In some odd way the commitment appears as if *ex nihilo*, bringing nothing but metaphysical confusion in its wake.[4]

It may be possible to restore the analogy, as follows. It is true that numbers contribute nothing to our understanding of boys, girls, and pairing, but they contribute a lot to our understanding of *language*. They are theoretical entities postulated to improve linguistic theory just as particles are postulated to improve physics. It may be true that, if all we want is a catalogue of the logical truths and valid arguments, we can avoid commitment. But if we want to explain these facts, and complete our semantics—including an account of how sentences link up to the world—we may have to fill out our picture of the world in various ways. In particular, if certain arguments turn on the logic of identity and quantifiers, we may have to provide singular terms with referents and quantifiers with domains in order to complete the semantics. The resulting postulations have the same justification which applies to corresponding moves in physical science. In effect, then, we are abandoning the type (A) argument which we found to be intuitively incredible, and replacing it with a type (B) argument which runs like this:

> The proposed semantic analysis of 'there are exactly as many boys as girls' (and related sentences) is ontologically committed to numbers.
> The postulation of numbers is theoretically successful (in the context of this semantics).
> Therefore, we have evidence that there are numbers and that the semantics is true.

We are not relying, as before, on the *truth* of a trivial observation together with a purely intra-linguistic study of logical relations, and then miraculously deriving the existence of controversial entities. We are doing theoretical semantics—including an account of the language-world tie—which may well require modifying our picture of the world.

---

[4] By 'our theory of John and his speed' I mean only such sentences as 'John ran' and 'John ran quickly'; whether numbers are needed for a complete scientific theory of motion and the like is, of course, a different question. Chapters VII and VIII take a first step toward answering the latter question also in the negative.

I think the analogy as repaired is cogent. But if this is the basis of the progressive uses of (*), then that use is open to a number of objections. First, it may be questioned whether the postulation of at least certain kinds of entities can play a role in improving our understanding of logic and semantics. For example, Michael Jubien has argued that the postulation of abstract entities as the satisfiers of predicates makes an explanatory account of satisfaction seem very unlikely.[5] Second, if the only reason we postulate those entities is to give an account of logic and semantics, then if we can produce an alternative account of logic and semantics which avoids those entities, there will be no more reason to postulate them. Thus the progressive use of (*) is based upon the extremely strong assumption that the only way to account for the logical implications of the sentences in question is to accord them the suggested logical form *and to interpret them semantically in such a way as to have them refer to those entities.* If in a given case the assumption is incorrect—if we can provide a successful semantics without the postulation—then (*) will no longer provide a short cut to ontological conclusions.

I believe that in some cases the assumption is false. In particular, there are cases in which it is possible to interpret the quantifiers of the sentences of the theory substitutionally and still provide a satisfactory account of their logic and semantics. Since substitutional quantification does not require the postulation of entities, (*) will not apply and arguments of type (A) will be shortcircuited. It also follows that (*) itself is incorrectly formulated. For, (*) holds as sufficient for commitment the fact that T logically implies '$(\exists x)Fx$', without specifying how '$(\exists x)$' is to be understood. Even if we acquiesce in the assignment of logical form which results in '$(\exists x)Fx$' as a consequence of T, if we withhold the objectual interpretation from '$(\exists x)$' we can avoid ontological commitment. Thus (*) should be reformulated to read:

(C)   T is ontologically committed to a/F's iff T logically implies '$(\exists x)(x = a)$'/'$(\exists x)Fx$' and '$(\exists x)$' is understood objectually.

One consequence of the move to (C) is a weakening of the progressive uses of the criterion. For, when we use (C) to interpret the second premiss of (A)-type arguments, that premiss becomes much harder to establish. We need to show not only that our assignment of

[5] Jubien, 1977.

logical form is the only one which correctly maps the implications in question, but also that we cannot—or at least should not—use the substitutional interpretation for the quantifiers. How could that be shown? We might argue that substitutional interpretation *should* not be used by showing directly that the entities in question exist, and hence that the objectual quantifier is the most reasonable semantic mechanism to use in talking about them. But this obviously affords no progress whatsoever in ontology: we would have to decide the onto-logical question in order to determine what semantics to use, and not vice versa. If we have a theory which is omega-inconsistent,[6] we know that the substitutional interpretation cannot be used. But this is very rarely the case.

In fact, it may now seem that where possible, substitutional quanti-fication is always preferable, and that this will automatically protect us from commitment to metaphysically troublesome entities. For, the theories which are thought to engender those commitments are rarely omega-inconsistent, and the entities in question never admit of convincing, independent proof—for that very reason we looked to arguments of type (A) for help. And now that we know how to avoid those commitments via substitutional quantification, we should by all means avoid them. I think that this suggestion is over optimistic due to its failure to reckon with the following conditions of applicability of substitutional quantification.

(1) Quantifiers cannot be interpreted substitutionally unless the language has or can be given expressions which can be taken as sub-stituends for the quantified variables. If a language has what look like quantifiers over propositions, we may be able to interpret these as sub-stitutional with respect to a certain class of sentences of the language (e.g. those without the quantifiers in question). But suppose a language has individual quantifiers and their variables, but has no singular terms? Or it may be the case that it has or can be given substituends for the variables, but not enough of them. Now here we must be careful: how many is enough? The answer is: as many as are needed to verify the substitutional rule for the quantifiers. That is, we must have enough substituends so that '$(\exists x)Fx$' is true iff some instance of 'Fx' is true; it is not required that we have a substituend for each entity. For example, we surely do not have a name for each real

---

[6] A theory is omega-inconsistent with respect to a set $S = \{s_1, \ldots, s_n, \ldots\}$ of substituends for a quantified variable x iff the theory has the following among its logical consequences: $\ulcorner \phi s_1 \urcorner, \ulcorner \phi s_2 \urcorner, \ldots, \ulcorner \phi s_n \urcorner, \ldots, \ulcorner (\exists x) \sim \phi x \urcorner$.

number, but we might have enough names so that any predicate which is satisfied by a real number is also satisfied by one with a name. Nevertheless, the need for enough substituends to verify the substitutional rule of the quantifiers is a non-trivial condition which must be met if substitutional quantification is to be used.

Furthermore, we must take care not to engender circularity in our choice of substituends. Saul Kripke has pointed out that this is a problem for defining substitutional quantification with respect to physical objects.[7] In order to have enough substituends we will have to appeal to definite descriptions: there are certainly not enough proper names to verify the substitutional interpretation. But if we add to our language an operator which forms a description for each open sentence, we will have an infinity of such descriptions, and we will need some kind of semantic analysis for them. The standard analysis—Russell's theory of descriptions—requires us to re-introduce the very quantifiers we were trying to explain! For example, if we explained '$(\exists x)(x$ is black)' as 'Some instance of 'x is black' is true', we might have to rely on such an instance as 'The book in the corner is black' to verify the original. But when we ask for the latter's semantics we would get '$(\exists x)((y)(y$ is a book in the corner $\equiv y=x)$ & x is black)', and we would have to explain '$(\exists x)$' and '(y)'. To deem them substitutional is circular; to deem them objectual re-introduces the very commitment we wanted to avoid. (This does not amount to a *proof* that substitutional quantification cannot be defined for physical objects, since it has not been shown that we could not introduce enough proper names to satisfy the substitution rule. Nevertheless, it makes such an eventuality rather unlikely. In any case, I am no advocate of substitutional quantification for physical objects: this is certainly a case of the conservative use of (*) since we are going to have physical objects anyway.)

(2) Even if condition (1) is met, substitutional quantification has not been shown a viable method for avoiding ontological commitment unless an adequate semantics can be provided for the atomic sentences of the language. This means that the atomic sentences must receive a semantical interpretation of their own which (a) meets all the constraints that apply to semantics in general; and (b) does not reinstate the very commitment we are trying to avoid. Under (a) we have the need for a finite account of the atomic sentences, and one which will show how those sentences are made true by the world. It is not enough

[7] Kripke, 1976, 379–81.

to declare that commitment has been avoided by stipulating the use of substitutional quantification and leaving the atomic sentences to get their truth conditions in some unspecified way. (b) reminds us that we must take care to avoid reference to the entities we are trying to avoid when we give the semantics of the atomic sentences. For example, it obviously will not do to interpret the substituends of the substitutional variables as names of the entities we are trying to avoid.

Conditions (1) and (2) make it clear that substitutional quantification cannot be used as an all-purpose panacea against unwanted ontological commitment. Instead, it is a strategy for building an alternative semantic interpretation of the sentences of a theory which in some cases may succeed in avoiding commitment. On the other hand, it is still correct to say that the progressive use of (A)-type arguments has been severely limited, since it will be very difficult in general to show that a satisfactory substitutional semantics cannot be worked out.

Let's sum up our findings to this point. Type (A) arguments rely on semantics to establish ontological commitment and thus ontological progress. In order to establish the second premiss of such arguments it must be argued that certain assignments of logical form and a certain kind of semantics—namely, one which requires reference to certain entities—are indispensable to the understanding of the sentences of the theory. This means that the progressive use of the criterion can be defeated in two ways: finding alternate logical forms, or finding alternate semantics. This makes the second premiss of type (A) arguments almost impossible to establish, and hence severely limits the progressive power of (C). On the other hand, requirements (1) and (2) make the provision of alternate semantics also very difficult; there are no easy ways to use semantics to settle ontological questions. The only solid link remaining between semantics and ontology seems to be this: if the *only* reason we have to believe in the existence of certain entities is that we are committed to them by sentences we cannot avoid asserting, we may *dispense* with those entities via a shift in logical form or semantics.

This account contrasts sharply with Donald Davidson's insistence that semantics is at the heart of ontology. He writes:

In sharing a language, in whatever sense this is required for communication, we share a picture of the world that must, in its large features, be true. It follows that in making manifest the large features of our language, we make manifest the large features of reality. One way of pursuing metaphysics is therefore to study the general structure of our language.[8]

Although this is only a programmatic opening to a closely argued and detailed discussion, probing this statement will reveal just how much can be explained and enforced in ontology through semantics. I will not stop to debate the truth of the first sentence; I am sceptical, but for argument's sake I will accept it. However, what can be meant by "large features" and "general structure" which language and the world are supposed to possess and which are supposed to be parallel in a mutually revealing fashion? On Davidson's own account of language, its structure is that of a first order theory: a set of expressions generated recursively from a finite list of primitive predicates and singular terms via quantifiers and truth-functions. The "large features" characterizing this structure seem to be: (i) the recursive generation of an infinity of sentences from a finite primitive vocabulary; (ii) the particular semantical properties of the generating mechanism, i.e., the quantifiers and the truth-functions; and (iii) the particular semantical properties of the primitive predicates and singular terms. To what "large features" of reality do these correspond? Reality is in no sense recursive—though perhaps a recursive model of our linguistic capabilities is somehow essential, and we are a part of reality. One might debate the existence of truth-functional combinations of "facts" if one were puzzled about how to interpret the truth-functions; but we are not so puzzled, nor is Davidson. On the other hand, the quantifiers, singular terms, and predicates *do* contribute a general feature of our picture of reality, namely that the world is a domain of entities which can support semantical relations such as satisfaction and reference. But, while this is non-trivial (and even debated by some), it hardly justifies any particular ontological conclusions. How then do the world and the large features of language connect?

On Davidson's account they connect as follows. The need to construe language within first order syntax and semantics puts certain global constraints on our primitive vocabulary, and it is the choice of primitive vocabulary which has direct ontological consequences. With a finite list of predicates and singular terms and the meagre resources of quantifiers and truth-functions we must do justice to natural language: this often requires violent paraphrase and restructuring of our native tongue. In certain cases, it may seem that the only way to

[8] Davidson, 1977, 244.

satisfy the global constraints is to adopt a particular logical form with its particular predicates and singular terms, and in its wake we will have ontological commitment. This is how Davidson views the genesis of commitment to events, for example. Now all the limitations in applying (C) to ontology apply to even this attenuated Davidsonian account. In order to reach the ontological conclusion it must be shown that (i) a certain logical form is indispensable; and (ii) the quantifiers involved in the form must be interpreted objectually. Under (ii) we must be satisfied (a) that the kind of entities which will result from the objectual interpretation *can* be used in an *explanatory* semantics, and that (b) a substitutional interpretation of the quantifiers is *impossible*. Subject to these limitations, how central is the "method of truth" to metaphysics? First, (ii) (a) may well require some independent ontologizing. Recall Jubien's argument that abstract entities cannot be used in explanatory semantics. A consequence of his argument is that whatever the needs of logical theory, we cannot use a logical form which will require objectual quantification with respect to abstracta since reference to abstracta is unintelligible. Thus we will have to do metaphysics before we can apply the "method" at all. Second, there is nothing in this picture which gives semantics a more central position than any other discipline. We need to have an account of our language and with that account may go certain theoretical commitments, which commitments can then be justified in much the way we justify similar commitments in other theories. But the same is equally true for physics, psychology, and so on: the theoretical needs of any discipline will have an impact on our ontology, and semantics will have to take its place along with the rest.

If there is nothing in the nature of the case to make semantics central to ontology, why then is it that so many important ontological applications seem to flow from semantics? The needs of language seem to be at the heart of the debates concerning the existence of universals, numbers, events, (Fregean) functions, types, substances, classes, time, etc. I think this line is shortsighted. It does not take account of the large contribution of the needs of other theories which are crucial in debating the existence of these entities—physics for numbers, classes, and properties (the last in an account of theoretical reduction), for example. It does not take account of the pretheoretical ontological stance which gives certain entities (a perhaps undeserved) legitimacy; we all accept classes and events in ordinary contexts and, if unawakened from our dogmatic slumber, will *require* our language to refer to these entities so that we can talk about and know them. It does not take account of the many ontological issues concerning which semantics is not fundamental; consider forces, fields, souls, pains, sense-data, impredicative sets, etc. Finally, the line does not take account of the fact that it is often very difficult to distinguish the needs of semantics from the needs of the portion of the world which the sentences in question describe. Is the preference of some for regions of space-time instead of ordinary objects in the description of change due to the needs of semantics or the nature of change? If we think the *Grosse Fugue* is an entity different from all its performances and scores, are we satisfying the needs of semantics or accommodating the nature of certain works of art? In both cases the answer is surely: both. To trumpet the centrality of semantics makes it appear as if we could clearly distinguish the respective contributions of semantics and the phenomena described. This, I think, we cannot do. Thus I find nothing in Davidson's argument which strengthens the connection between semantics and ontology beyond the tenuous link described above.

From this perspective, we can evaluate one of Quine's recurring complaints against the use of substitutional quantification in avoiding ontological commitment.[9] To declare that our quantifiers should be understood substitutionally is to abstract from reference altogether, says Quine. Until the language in question is provided with a referential interpretation, we cannot tell which expressions are intended to refer and which are to play other semantical roles; thus the ontological commitments of the sentences in the language are not determined. Quine's point here is essentially correct, but put misleadingly. It is true that, until we have a semantics for language which shows how the world makes its sentences true, we will not understand the language. It is true that the only programme known to make progress on the project is referential semantics—semantics which *bases* itself on denotation, satisfaction, and objectual quantification. Thus the tie of our language to the world will *ultimately* rely upon reference. But this is no reason not to use substitutional quantification (nor does Quine intend it to be). It is not required that all quantifiers be explained objectually in order to tie sentences to the world. It is sufficient that the connection of a sentence with a substitutional quantifier to the world be explained via reference *at some point*, but this point need not be the sentence itself. Compare truth-functions. In

[9] Quine, 1973 [42], 112, 136.

a fully referential language, how is 'John fell and Peter laughed' tied to the world? We say that it is true iff 'John fell' and 'Peter laughed' are both true and then we display the connection of 'John fell' and 'Peter laughed' via denotation and satisfaction relations. That is, the language–world tie of the conjunction is mediated by that of its conjuncts. In general, if the truth condition of a sentence is given in terms of other sentences, it is then sufficient if the latter have their tie to the world clearly displayed for this virtue to accrue to the original as well. Now this is precisely the case of substitutional quantification. The truth of a substitutionally quantified sentence is equivalent to the truth of all (or one) of its instances, and so it suffices for reference to tie the instances to the world. Thus the truth in Quine's point comes to this: one cannot use substitutional quantification in place of referential semantics altogether—at some point reference must be used to root our language in the world. But this can be admitted and still sub-stitutional quantification can be used to avoid ontological commit-ment, if conditions (1) and (2) can be met.

This chapter (and the rest of this book) rests on the assumption that substitutional quantification is ontologically neutral—that its use does not automatically confer existence on entities to which the sub-stituends of the quantifiers (supposedly) refer. Charles Parsons has challenged this neutrality:

The fact that the substitution interpretation yields truth conditions for quantified sentences means that everything necessary for speaking of entities is present, and the request for some more absolute verification of their existence seems senseless.[10]

This claim is a very surprising one. The truth conditions for substitutionally quantified sentences do not appear to require the existence of an entity to guarantee truth (putting aside doubts about the need for existent expressions to substitute for the quantified variable). For example, we naturally expect that if quantification is interpreted substitutionally,

   $(\exists x)$(the museum has a statute of x)

may be true even if the museum's only statue is a statue of Zeus.

Parsons supports his claim by responding to Quine's charge that substitutional quantification is irrelevant to ontology. Quine argued

[10] Parsons, 1971 [33], 234.

that (a) since substitutional quantification is explicable in terms of truth and substitution no matter what the substitution class—even that whose sole member is the left-hand parenthesis—we must deny that it carries existential import. For we surely do not have to provide an entity for the left-hand parenthesis to name in order to count true those sentences which contain it. And (b) "... we [cannot] introduce any control by saying that only substitutional quantification in the substitution class of singular terms is to count as a version of existence ... [because] the very notion of singular terms appeals implicitly to ... objectual quantification."[11] Parsons replies to (a) by pointing out two formal features of substitutional quantification with respect to singular terms which he thinks can be used to distinguish that substitution class from other (trivial) ones. They are the fact that that class "admits identity with the property of substitutivity *salva veritate*. [And] it has infinitely many members that are distinguishable by the identity relation." I find this appeal unconvincing. The role of identity in a substitutionally interpreted language is quite different from its ordinary role (as Parsons himself seems to recognize in his footnote 8). As Ruth Marcus pointed out,[12] identity will be replaced by a series of syntactically defined substitution principles depending for their scope on the expressive richness of the language. We may expect such principles for predicates and operators in addition to singular terms, and there seems to be no reason why we could not have them for marks of punctuation as well. This suffices to cast doubt on both features to which Parsons appeals, for any expressions for which we formulate such principles could belong to an infinite class of expressions which are distinguished by those principles.

Parsons's response to (b) is to

concede Quine's point . . . for a certain central core class of singular terms, which we might suppose to denote objects whose existence we do not expect to explicate by substitutional quantification. We might then make certain analogical extensions of the class of singular terms in such a way that they are related to quantifications construed as substitutions. The criterion for "genuine reference" is given in other terms.[13]

But this is not sufficient. Consider the problem with which Quine began. We speak informal English containing proper names, phrases

---

[11] Quine, 1968 [40], 106.
[12] Marcus, 1963.
[13] Parsons, 1971 [33], 233.

of the form "the . . .", and other expressions paraphrasable into the latter. Sometimes we use these expressions as if they denoted existent objects (or as if we thought they did) and sometimes we do not. Evidently, the mere assertion of a sentence containing such an expression does not commit the speaker to the existence of an object named by that expression; what then does? Quine's answer, in essence, was this: we choose a locution of informal English which is unquestionably referential, and hence unquestionably sufficient for ontological commitment, and symbolize it '$(\exists x)$'. Then we translate everyone's remarks into a formal language incorporating '$(\exists x)$' and a formal logic. Finally, we commit ourselves ontologically by asserting sentences *in the formal language* which have logical consequences formulated in terms of '$(\exists x)$'. Notice that there is no pretence to an *explication* of existence. Rather, by choosing a locution which we simply recognize as existentially committing and passing to a formal language we get a symbolic *symptom* of ontological commitment. Now what is accomplished by Parsons's "analogical extensions"? We may have sufficient reason to classify the new substituends with the singular terms *syntactically*—they replace the same variables, and so on. But it is their semantical interpretation which is in question: do they denote? For an answer to this question Quine urges us to consult the quantifier. And Parsons seems to agree, for he seems to think of substitutional quantification as supplying an *explication* of existence for the denotata of class abstracts. But when we consult the truth conditions for the *substitutionally interpreted* quantifier we find a studious neutrality in this regard. What kind of notion of existence is it that provides for the truth of existentially quantified sentences without requiring a non-empty universe?

Perhaps Parsons is relying on the presumption that the meta-language quantifiers are objectual and so the truth condition for quantified sentences engenders commitment to expression-types. This would explain why he limits his theory to what he calls "linguistic" abstract entities, e.g., propositions, attributes, and extensions of predicates. If this is what Parsons intends, then perhaps his "expli-cation" of existence for these entities goes as follows. Ordinary existence is what is required for the truth of existentially quantified sentences, when the quantifier is interpreted in the ordinary manner. *Linguistic existence*—a name for what Parsons is explicating if this interpretation of his intentions is correct—is what is required for the truth of existentially quantified sentences, when the quantifier is interpreted substitutionally *in an objectual meta-language*. Thus '$(\exists F)_s Fa$' expresses the "linguistic existence" of properties because it is interpreted by '$(\exists F)_0$ ⌜Fa⌝ is true' in the meta-language. But then what is the difference between the linguistic existence of properties and the ordinary existence of predicates? From the point of view of ontological commitment there is none, and it is misleading to call it a new sense of existence and announce it as a metaphysical innovation.

Furthermore, Timothy McCarthy has pointed out that even this weakened reading of Parsons's claim is open to objection. For, it amounts to reading into a sentence S of the object language the semantical structure and ontological commitments of the meta-linguistic interpretation of ⌜'S' is true⌝, and this is illegitimate. 'Cats meow or dogs growl' is interpreted by ''Cats meow' is true or 'Dogs growl' is true'; but the fact that the latter is committed to the existence of sentences does not show that 'Cats meow or dogs growl' is so committed. Likewise, the fact that '$(\exists F)_s Fa$' is interpreted as '$(\exists F)_0$ ⌜Fa⌝ is true' and the latter is committed to the existence of predicates does not show that '$(\exists F)_s Fa$' is so committed. Thus even if we take "linguistic existence" seriously, it affects only the commitments of the meta-language in giving the semantics of the object language; the ontological neutrality of substitutional quantification in the object language is utterly unaffected.

Similarly, if the following remarks by Michael Dummett are intended to challenge that neutrality, they must be rejected:

There remains this difference between schematic letters and variables, that variables always require us to specify the totality over which they range ... substitutional quantification is not a genuine alternative to 'ontic' quantification ... The advocates of substitutional quantification share with Quine the assumption that ontological commitment is required only by 'ontic' quantification, and therefore regard substitutional quantification as a means of achieving liberation from ontological commitment. Both are wrong, because it is not quantification which in the first place requires the ascription of reference: reference must be ascribed to any expressions which function as significant units of sentences of a language ...[14]

Now Dummett recognizes two senses of 'reference': (i) the relation of naming; (ii) semantic role. In sense (ii) the end of the quotation is correct: quantifiers are not more central to the ascription of semantic role than are sentential connectives or predicates. But it is obvious that

[14] Dummett, 1973, 526–8.

the question of ontological commitment turns on sense (i) of reference: the decision to interpret a significant unit of language *as a name* or a quantifier *as objectual* is the decision which has ontological consequences. Thus the end of the quotation does not support the rest, which is in fact false. It is true that the declaration that a quantifier is substitutional must be accompanied by a semantic interpretation of *sentences formed by replacing the quantified variable with each of its substituends*. But this does not commit us to interpreting the *substituends themselves* as names. Indeed, by using an extended sense of "definition in context" (developed in detail in the next chapter), we may avoid assigning the substituends any independent semantic role. We may rather interpret the sentences in question as wholes in which the substituends do not play any clearly delineated role. The extent to which ontological commitment is avoided depends upon the nature of that interpretation. As we shall see, this strategy can be very fruitful in reducing ontology.

IV

Semantics for Languages With Substitutional Quantification

Ontological commitment for a theory T is wholly determined by the semantics of T: once we know how to interpret T's quantifiers, and logical implication is defined for T's sentences, T's commitments are fixed. In this chapter I will describe a general approach to the semantics of languages with substitutional quantification and contrast it with Davidsonian views on semantics in general and with Kripke's views concerning substitutional semantics in particular. Since I am not undertaking to provide a complete philosophical foundation for semantics, certain fundamental assumptions concerning the nature of semantics will be made without argument. It is agreed by all that a finitary assignment of meanings to the sentences of a language provides an adequate semantic interpretation of that language. Controversy centres around the question: What are meanings? I am assuming that the meaning of a sentence is its truth condition. But I must explicitly dissociate myself from Davidson's view that the only constraint on the provision of truth conditions is that Tarski equivalences be deducible from the assignment. In my opinion this condition is neither necessary nor sufficient. I will not argue for my view, but just briefly indicate my reasons and then press on to the subject of this chapter.

The condition is not necessary because (i) as Kripke has pointed out, we may have perfectly acceptable truth conditions for all the sentences of a language and yet the deduction of the Tarski equivalences is blocked by some completely irrelevant factor,[1] and (ii) I can see no reason why an acceptable theory of truth must deductively determine the extension of 'true' any more than an acceptable theory of horses must determine the extension of 'horse'. This means that I do not buy the characterization of the Tarski equivalences as the basic facts that a theory of truth (alone) has to explain.

[1] Kripke, 1976, 338–9.

That the deducibility condition is not sufficient is recognized even by Davidson since that would legitimize the one-line definition of truth:[2]

(D) $(S)_0(S$ is true-in-L iff $(\exists T)_s(S='T'$ & $T))$

where 'S' is an *objectual* variable over L's sentences and 'T' is a *substitutional* variable taking L's sentences as substituends. Now Davidson rules this out by fiat, declaring that this results in an "uninteresting" definition of truth.[3] Thus the condition he claims to be sufficient is that the T-equivalences be deducible *and* that the definition not be (D). Needless to say, the elimination of (D) needs some kind of motivation other than an expression of lack of interest. One characteristic of (D) which does make it less interesting and fruitful than, say, the classical Tarskian truth definition, is that (D) does not reveal the subsentential semantic structure of L with which logical relations can be explained and which helps to account for our potentially infinite linguistic abilities. However, as Fodor has pointed out, it is not clear that it is the job of the theory of *truth* to do this, rather than another department of semantics—e.g., formal logic as a theory of the relation of formal truth guarantees among sentences.[4] And in any case, we could have the best of both worlds by marrying Tarski and (D), as follows. We use the usual Tarskian recursive analysis of the quantifiers and connectives. In order to define satisfaction for the primitive predicates, we mimic (D) using a substitutional variable 'F' taking primitive predicates of L as substituends:

(D*) $(f)(s)(s$ satisfies f in L iff $(\exists F)_s(f='F'$ & $F\bar{s}))$

where 'f' is objectual over L's primitive predicates, 's' is objectual over sequences, and 'F$\bar{s}$' takes as substituend the result of replacing each occurrence of a free variable x_i of (the substituend of) 'F' with the appropriate individual constant s_i designating the ith member of s.[5] (Note that Tarski + (D*) provides only a theory of truth, not a

---

[2] Marcus, 1963, 246–7 and n. 10.

[3] Davidson's literal requirement bars taking all the T-equivalences as axioms of a truth theory by demanding that the truth theory be finitely axiomatized; see Davidson, 1970, 178. Since (D) is a single sentence, it meets the letter of this requirement, but clearly misses its spirit: interesting theories are ones which reveal the "recursive structure" of the language (see Davidson, 1967, 310, and Davidson, 1973 [29], 81), and (D) has nothing to say about this.

[4] Fodor, 1972, 48–50.

[5] Of course, such constants are not always available. But by considering (D*) in a setting in which they are, we can evaluate Davidson's constraints.

definition; but this is all that Davidson now requires.) The Tarski half of this team gives us the "recursive structure" of L, while (D*) completes the theory of truth by making the T-equivalences deducible. And the possibility of using (D*) to this end has important consequences: it removes the restriction to a finite number of primitive predicates! For, that restriction was motivated only by the thought that for each primitive predicate we will need a separate clause in the theory of truth, and hence if we had an infinity of them we could not have a finite theory. (D*) shows how to frame a finite theory without any commitment to how many primitive predicates there are. Of course, it may be argued that as the basis for a theory of truth, (D*) is pitifully weak: how much headway does it allow us to make towards the explanation of how the world makes our sentences true and false—i.e., towards settling the perennial problem of how language and the world connect? Very little. But then exactly the same is true for the Tarski definition of satisfaction.[6] In fact, their contributions to our overall theory of language are *identical*, since (D*) does nothing more than to collect all of Tarski's separate clauses into one sentence. It might be argued that if we allow an infinity of primitive predicates and rely upon (D*) for a finite theory of truth we will lose the intimate connection between the theory of truth and our account of what it is to understand the language.[7] This, I think, does close the door on (D*); however, this is a far cry from supporting the requirement that the T-equivalences be deducible.

Thus the appeal to the deducibility of the T-equivalences is not the criterion of the success of the assignment of truth conditions to the sentences of a language, and cannot be the basis of a philosophical account of the role of truth conditions in our overall theory of language. Rather, if the truth condition of a sentence is to play the role of its meaning, then it must be possible to use that truth condition to explain everything which the meaning of a sentence is expected to explain. Included in this group are: the explanation of linguistic competence and communication, the explanation of language learning, and the explanation of the various types of acts which can be performed via the use of language. In other words, truth conditions must be capable of playing the central theoretical role in a comprehensive theory of language: all facets of language which such a theory explains will be explained by starting with the truth conditions of sentences and

[6] Field, 1972.   [7] Dummett, 1973, 458.

adapting them to the particular context via fixed procedures.[8] Thus truth conditions will be for sentences what the subatomic structure of an element is for that element: just as the subatomic structure of an element is the basis for explaining that element's physical and chemical properties via the application of laws concerning the behaviour of sub-atomic particles and their interactions, so the truth condition of a sentence will determine what it can be used to communicate, how it is learned, what linguistic acts can be performed with it, and so on, via fixed rules which express the general relations between truth conditions and these other matters. Truth conditions are meanings only if they can play this role. I shall assume that they can; hence I shall describe the provision of semantics for a language in terms of providing its sentences with truth conditions.

By *a language L with substitutional quantification* I will under-stand a language which can be finitely partitioned into mutually exclusive sets of sentences L0, L1, . . . , Ln meeting the following conditions. L0 contains only quantifiers, truth-functions, singular terms, and predicates. Thus L0 is a fully referential language, and its truth conditions are assigned in the usual manner. Li is constructed from Li − 1 by adding substitutional quantifiers new to L0 ∪ L1 ∪ . . . ∪ Li − 1. This can be done in the following ways. (i) New substitutional variables and their quantifiers are introduced; the sub-stituends for the variables are expressions of Li − 1, and the contexts of quantification are the contexts of Li − 1 in which the substituends occur. Example: add substitutional quantifiers with respect to the sentences of Li − 1 where the latter may occur in the truth functional contexts of Li − 1. (ii) New substitutional variables and their quantifiers are introduced and the substituends are drawn from Li − 1, but the expressions which are the contexts of quantification are new to Li. Example: add substitutional quantifiers with respect to the sentences of Li − 1 and stipulate that the contexts of quantification be new sentential contexts—e.g., if Li − 1 is an extensional language, the new contexts may be propositional attitudes or modal operators. (iii) New substitutional variables and their quantifiers are introduced and new expressions are introduced to be their substituends; however, the contexts of quantification come from Li − 1. Example: let Li − 1 be a referential language which admits no empty singular terms (i.e., such that '$(\exists x)_0(x = a)$' is provable for each singular term 'a') and add substitutional variables taking as substituends terms of the form

[8] Dummett, 1973, 456–7.

'(ix)...x...' which may be empty. These "singular terms" will occupy the same positions as genuinely referring singular terms in Li − 1. (iv) New substitutional variables and their quantifiers are introduced in Li, and both the substituends and the contexts of quantification are new to Li. Example: the addition of virtual class theory with substitutional quantifiers to a language Li − 1 possessing no set-theoretical vocabulary. Both the context '... ∈ —' and the class abstracts which are the substituends of the variables are new to Li.

The assignment of truth conditions to the sentences of Li will depend upon which of the four methods for introducing substitutional quantification into Li was used. We may assume that the sentences of Li − 1 have already been assigned their truth conditions. Li is handled as follows. (i) In this case the truth rules for the substitutional quantifiers suffice to determine the truth conditions for all sentences of Li since all the unquantified sentences of Li are sentences of Li − 1, and hence already have truth conditions. (ii)–(iv) Since the contexts of quantification are new to Li the unquantified sentences of Li are also new to Li. Their truth conditions must be given in terms of the sentences of L0 ∪ ... ∪ Li − 1. *Any finite method of accomplishing this is acceptable.* In practice we typically use a correlation of the unquantified sentences of Li with sentences of Li − 1 (where the latter are *not* unquantified sentences of Li − 1 but possess rich structure). And while it is to be expected that the correlation will be effected via an analysis of the structure of the unquantified sentences of Li, there is no reason to expect that this analysis will follow the lines of custom dictated by the ordinary referential analysis of the structure of such sentences. For example, Russell's theory of descriptions suggests the following correlation for the case of type (iii):

'$\phi((\text{i}x) \ldots x \ldots)$' is true iff '$(\exists x)(y)(\ldots y \ldots \equiv y=x \,\&\, \phi x)$' is true.

It will be helpful to have an example of a language L interpreted according to my lights. The following is an example of type (iv). L0 may be any referentially interpreted language. L1 contains the substitutional variables 'a', 'b', 'c', . . . and their quantifiers; the substituends for the substitutional variables, viz., all expressions of the form '$\{x: \ldots x \ldots\}$' where '... x ...' is replaced by an open sentence of L0 whose only free variable is x; and the symbol '∈' which syntactically is a dyadic predicate letter, taking substitutional variables or class abstracts to the right, and variables or singular terms of L0 to the left. L = L0 ∪ L1. The sentences of L0 receive truth conditions in the classical manner; the substitutionally quantified sentences of L1 receive truth conditions in terms of the unquantified sentences of L1 via the usual recursive rules; and the unquantified sentences of L1 receive truth conditions in terms of the sentences of L0 via the following rule:

(C) $\alpha \in \{x: \ldots x \ldots\}$ has the same semantic interpretation as $\ulcorner \ldots \alpha \ldots \urcorner$

where α may be either a singular term or variable of L0, and $\ulcorner \ldots \alpha \ldots \urcorner$ is the result of substituting α for 'x'. When α is a singular term of L0, (C) provides that the sentence $\ulcorner \alpha \in \{x: \ldots x \ldots\} \urcorner$ receive the same truth condition as the sentence $\ulcorner \ldots \alpha \ldots \urcorner$; when α is a variable of L0, (C) provides that the open sentence $\ulcorner \alpha \in \{x: \ldots x \ldots\} \urcorner$ receive the same satisfaction conditions as the open sentence $\ulcorner \ldots \alpha \ldots \urcorner$. To illustrate the semantics of L, let 'x is a horse' and 'Sam' be respectively a predicate and a singular term of L0. In L1 we have the sentence

(1)   (a)$((\exists x) x \in a \supset Sam \in a)$.

It is true iff all of its instances are, one of which is

(2) $(\exists x)(x \in \{x: x \text{ is a horse}\}) \supset Sam \in \{x: x \text{ is a horse}\}$.

(2) is what I call an unquantified sentence of L1 since it contains none of the quantifiers specific to L1; its truth condition is given by (C). For, if we apply (C) to its antecedent and the consequent, we see that (2) has the same truth condition as

(3) $(\exists x)(x \text{ is a horse}) \supset Sam \text{ is a horse}$,

and (3) is a sentence of L0 whose truth condition is supposed given.

(It is worth pointing out that for the sake of the simplicity of the example I have eliminated a refinement due to Charles Parsons which would greatly increase the power and interest of L.[9] Namely, I have not allowed the open sentences in the class abstracts to have free variables other than the variable of the abstract itself. If this more liberal course is taken a slight change in (C) is required. In my treatment of arithmetic in Part II I will employ a parallel liberalization and formulate its semantics explicitly.)

The first comparison is with what I will call Davidsonian semantics. However, I explicitly disclaim any implication that what I shall

[9] Parsons, 1971 [33], 235.

describe is or ever was endorsed by Davidson in precisely the form and with all the strength here given. Nevertheless, I think the following represents a framework for semantics which is inspired by Davidson's writings, and in terms of which many people have come to think owing to his influence. According to Davidsonian semantics, the type of semantical interpretation an expression receives is determined by its syntactical status. The two chief syntactical divisions are between primitive and non-primitive expressions, and among the former between operators and non-operators. The class of sentences of the language is defined by explaining how the operators attach first to other primitive expressions, and then to complex expressions, to form sentences. In first order languages the singular terms and (primitive) predicates are primitive non-operators, and the quantifiers and sentential connectives are primitive operators. Now the semantical interpretation of syntactically primitive expressions bifurcates along the same line. Primitive non-operators receive as their semantical interpretation some direct language–world tie which then serves as the basis for the truth relation between sentences and the world. (This direct tie is sometimes itself eliminated via Tarski so as to become the basis for a *definition* of truth.) Primitive operators receive recursive rules which map the semantical interpretation of the expression to which they attach onto the semantical interpretation of the expression which results from the attachment. Thus the semantically primitive and the syntactically primitive expressions coincide. Furthermore, each primitive expression receives its own semantical rule which describes the contribution it makes to the truth conditions of the sentences in which it appears. Thus it makes sense to ask for the meaning of each syntactically primitive expression, if we are careful not to reify meanings but rather to be satisfied with an account of the expression's contribution to truth.

Davidson defines a semantically primitive expression as one which appears in a sentence whose truth condition is not given by all the rules which give the truth conditions of all the sentences in which the expression does not appear.[10] Thus semantical primitiveness is relative to the semantical rules with which the language is interpreted (as it should be): two semantical interpretations of the same language which assign the same truth conditions to the same sentences may nevertheless differ as to which expressions are semantically primitive. This

---

[10] Davidson, 1965.

definition accords well with the characterization of meaning as contribution to truth. It also fits the provision of each primitive expression with its own meaning rule; for if the rules giving truth conditions to all sentences in which an expression e does not appear do not suffice to cover at least some sentences in which e does appear, then apparently what is missing is an account of what e contributes to the truth conditions of the sentences in which it appears, and such an account will be the meaning rule for e.

A further characteristic of Davidsonian semantics is *strong componentialism*. Componentialism (*simpliciter*) requires that the semantic interpretation of a non-primitive expression depend upon the semantic interpretations of its components, i.e., its sub-expressions; the strong variety requires further that the semantic interpretation of a non-primitive expression be independent of the semantic interpretations of all expressions other than its components. First order languages exemplify strong componentialism. The truth condition of a sentence composed solely of a predicate and singular terms is a function of the denotata of the singular terms and the extension of the predicate; the case for truth functional combinations is obvious; and a quantified sentence's truth condition is a function of the extension of its open sentence and the truth rule for its quantifier. But it is also clear that any language interpreted in accordance with the "one primitive—one rule" policy using rules which do not give the semantic interpretation of a particular expression in terms of the interpretations of other particular expressions, will be strongly componential. For, the rules for the primitives determine their contributions to the truth conditions of the sentences in which they appear; thus the set of all the rules for all the primitives in a given sentence must suffice to determine that sentence's truth conditions. Since the rules give the semantic interpretation of each expression independently from the others, the truth condition of a given sentence is independent of the semantics of the rest of the language: the semantical interpretation of any expression not in the sentence may be changed without affecting the truth condition of the sentence.

Finally, we may note a consequence of strong componentialism for logic. Davidson's view is that logical truth is truth determined by the semantics for the primitive operators. Whether or not this is precisely the case, it certainly seems to be true that a complete semantics for a language—i.e., an assignment of truth conditions to its sentences—will contain enough information to determine logical truth for the language. Now it is a consequence of strong componentialism that logical truth for a sentence can be determined solely on the basis of the semantical interpretation of the sub-expressions of that sentence, and likewise entailment can be determined solely on the basis of the semantics of the sub-expressions of sentences involved.

This completes the sketch of some of the main features of what I am here calling Davidsonian semantics. How does the Davidsonian framework relate to the description of semantics for a language with substitutional quantification? Consider the language L of substitutionally quantified virtual class theory. What are the semantical primitives of its component L1? The substitutional quantifiers of L1 and its truth-functions qualify, *but the class abstracts do not*! For, if we consider all the rules which are needed to determine the truth conditions of sentences in which no abstracts appear, then we must include those rules needed to assign truth conditions to purely quantified sentences. But since the quantifiers are substitutional, the truth condition for a purely quantified sentence is given in terms of the truth conditions for its instances—and those *do* contain abstracts. And thus to assign truth conditions to the purely quantified sentences we will need to use the rules for sentences in which abstracts appear—in fact, we shall need *all* the rules of the semantics. Thus the rules which suffice to assign truth conditions to sentences in which abstracts do not appear *are* also sufficient to determine the truth conditions for the sentences in which abstracts do appear, and hence abstracts are not semantically primitive. This is characteristic of substitutional quantification: the substituends are never semantically primitive according to the Davidsonian definition. And this consequence holds independently of the ultimate semantical interpretation of the substituends. It makes no difference whether in L1 we add a correlation to a lower level, as I did above, or we interpret the abstracts as names of sets, or choose a third way. Furthermore, if we add substitutional quantification in L1 with respect to the open sentences of L0, then even the intuitively primitive predicates of L0 will cease to be primitive: the rules needed to give the truth conditions for '(F)Fa' may include all the rules for the language, and hence all the rules for the "primitive" predicates.

Second, notice that the semantics for L are not strongly componential. This too is characteristic of substitutional quantification: the truth condition of a substitutionally quantified sentence depends upon the truth conditions of its instances, and these contain expressions which are not sub-expressions of the original sentence. If we change the semantical interpretation of one of those expressions which are foreign to the original sentence we may indeed change the truth conditions of the sentence. Likewise, it *may* be the case that logical relations can be changed by altering parts of the language other than the expressions found in the sentences to be related. (Whether or not this will occur depends upon how we decide to define logical consequence for such languages.)

Third, the dovetailing of the semantical and syntactical primitives is absent from the semantics for L. The syntactical primitives include the set abstraction operator, which is not semantically primitive for Davidson. Of course, it is not semantically complex either: primitive/complex will not be an exhaustive division of the expressions of L. Likewise the "one primitive—one rule" feature of Davidsonian semantics is inapplicable in this context. Such expressions as '∈' and the abstraction operator do not receive rules which give their semantic interpretations. To the question: What does '∈' mean?—we do not receive even a de-entified answer.

What is the significance of the fact that the semantics for L do not fit the Davidsonian framework? The Davidsonian framework is too narrow. The semantics for L do all that a Davidsonian can ask: a finite list of rules is given which effectively assigns to each sentence of L its truth condition. What the Davidsonian framework does is to place severe restrictions on the *form* this assignment can take. But, it seems to me that these restrictions have only the force of custom, not necessity. There is nothing about the contributions of truth conditions to a theory of meaning which requires strong componentialism, one semantical rule per primitive, and so on. And the best way to see this is by appeal to substitutional quantification in general and L in particular: they are admitted as semantically unproblematic by all.

If we jettison the Davidsonian framework, what do we put in its place? NOTHING. What is wrong with the framework is not that it picked the wrong restrictions, but rather that it invented restrictions where there ought to be *none*. *All* that is required is a finite, effective assignment of truth conditions. We should recognize that the semantic interpretation of a sentence may be strongly dependent upon the semantic interpretation of other parts of the language. We should recognize that there may be no answer whatsoever to the question: What does (some expression) e mean?—other than to point out a whole bunch of semantical rules (which may include all the rules for the language). In different cases the semantical roles of syntactically primitive expressions may be very complex and highly context dependent. But each case will have to be described separately, and I cannot conceive of any useful generalizations in this area. In general, the unquantified sentences of a level Li in the partition will be given truth conditions via the sentences of the level $Li - 1$, and this will require some kind of analysis of that class of sentences on the basis of the syntactically primitive expressions which compose them. But this may be done recursively, or by some finite classification whose form cannot be dictated beforehand.

One consequence of abandoning the Davidsonian framework is that semantics becomes more complicated. Before, given any sentence, it was possible to give a complete description of the semantics of the sentence via the semantic interpretation of its primitive subexpressions. For a substitutionally quantified sentence we must give enough of a description of the rest of the language so as to trace a route from it to the world. Furthermore, the relations of a single sentence to various other parts of the language may turn on independent factors in its semantics, thus requiring a complex description of those semantics. For example, consider the sentence

(4)   Sam $\in$ {x: x is a horse},

and, in particular, the role of '$\in$'. On the one hand, (4) logically implies

(5) $(\exists a)(Sam \in a)$.

How do we account for this implication? By citing the truth conditions of '$(\exists x)$' in (5) and the fact that (4) is an instance of (5). In spelling this out, '$\in$' will be classified syntactically as dyadic: it takes singular terms and variables from L0 on the left and class abstracts and (substitutional) variables from L1 on the right. Thus from the point of view of the logic of L1, we may say that (4) has the form 'a R b', as long as it is understood that that form is meant only as part of the account of its logical relations to substitutionally quantified sentences of L1. When we turn to the relations (4) has to the sentences of L0, and to its ultimate truth conditions—the ultimate account of how (4) links up with the world—we describe it quite differently. Via the correlation (C), (4) has the same truth condition as 'Sam is a horse', and so from the point of view of L0 and the world, (4) has the form 'Fa'. This latter form indicates how referential semantics will root (4) in the world, and also how it will relate logically to the other sentences of L0.

We saw that Davidson's definition of semantical primitive is inapplicable to languages with substitutional quantification. Nevertheless there are intuitive differences between various groups of expressions of such languages: the standard primitives of L0, the newly introduced expressions at each higher level, and the sentences which can be compounded out of both, differ in semantically important ways. Some of these differences may be captured in the following two definitions. An expression e in a language L receives a *direct interpretation* by a set R of rules of interpretation iff there is a sentence S(e) containing an occurrence of e such that the rules R do not give the truth conditions for S(e) wholly in terms of the semantical interpretation of other expressions of L. The idea is that an expression receives a direct interpretation (is *semantically direct* for short) if it is interpreted via a direct language–world tie; it is semantically indirect if it is interpreted as mediating between the semantical interpretations of other expressions of L. As examples, let's compare disjunction with a primitive predicate. 'S ∨ T' is true iff 'S' is true or 'T' is true; this interpretation of '∨' makes it a link between the truth conditions of various sentences (disjunctions and their disjuncts). Its function is wholly intra-linguistic. By contrast, 'Fa' is true iff the object denoted by 'a' satisfies 'F': the rule which describes the semantic contribution of a primitive predicate gives its satisfaction condition, and that condition relates the predicate to extra-linguistic reality. In a language with substitutional quantification the primitive predicates and singular terms and objectual quantifiers of L0 are semantically direct; all other expressions are semantically indirect. The importance of the direct/ indirect distinction is clear when we reflect that one of the purposes of a semantical interpretation is to display enough of the way in which sentences relate to the world so that we can formulate the conditions under which each sentence will be true. The recursive structure of the interpretation requires that some sentences be tied directly to the world—i.e., without the mediation of other sentences. Once a sufficient basis of this kind is laid down, we can proceed with various methods of compounding sentences without worrying about the language–world tie, as long as the methods of compounding create a well-defined truth dependence between the new sentences and the old. It is the first stage which is fraught with philosophical perplexities; the second is relatively unproblematic. This difference is recorded by the direct/indirect distinction.

Secondly, we feel a strong contrast between all those expressions which the semantical rules mention explicitly and those which are not so mentioned: the latter are viewed as dependent upon the former for their semantic interpretation. If an expression is mentioned explicitly in the rules then its contribution to the interpretation of the expressions in which it occurs is viewed as unanalysable: it requires explicit description in the rules. If an expression is not so mentioned, then its semantic interpretation is viewed as analysable in terms of the semantic interpretation of other expressions and their (syntactic) relations to it. We may call those expressions mentioned in the rules *semantically independent* and the others *semantically dependent*. The independent/dependent distinction can be drawn in terms of what the rules say, as above. Typically, an expression will be semantically independent iff it is syntactically primitive; all of the standard primitives of L0 and all of the newly introduced expressions of the higher levels are semantically independent. Here we see a new dovetailing of syntax and semantics which expresses the Davidsonian intuition in the context of languages with substitutional quantification. And it is here (if anywhere) that Davidson's proof of the need for a finite semantical interpretation for a language on the grounds that finite beings understand the language. Assuming (as he does) that the rules of interpretation express what we know when we understand the language, we can conclude that the rules must be finite. From this it follows that the number of semantically independent expressions must be finite.

Finally, we should note the place of so-called "inductive definitions" in languages with substitutional quantification. Conventional wisdom has it that these are not really definitions since the hallmark of a real definition is the eliminability of the definiendum by the definiens in all contexts, and "inductive definitions" do not provide this. For example, while the equations

(A) $(x)(x\cdot 0 = 0)$
       $(x)(y)(x\cdot y' = x\cdot y + x)$

suffice to eliminate '·' in favour of the prime, '0', '+', etc. when surrounded by numerals, it fails when '·' is flanked by variables, as in

(B) $(x)(y)(x\cdot y = y\cdot x)$

and so (A) does not *define* '·'. From the point of view of semantics, this means that (A) cannot be taken as adequate to introduce '·' into a language since there are sentences in the language containing '·' whose truth conditions are not fixed by the totality of semantical rules for the language together with (A). The semantical significance of a "real definition" is that universal eliminability is achieved iff all sentences containing the new expression will receive truth conditions via the "definition", and thus eliminability becomes the *sine qua non* of definition—or so it was thought. In languages with substitutional quantification this equivalence no longer holds; it is often possible to give a complete semantical interpretation of an expression via an "inductive definition" if that expression is being introduced in Li (i > 0) as a context of substitutional quantification. For example, imagine a language which already contains successor and addition—i.e., all sentences whose non-logical primitives are just '′' and '+' already have their truth conditions assigned. Then (A) suffices to assign truth conditions to all occurrences of '·' flanked by numerals, and the substitutional interpretation of the quantifiers suffices to extend the interpretation to all other sentences in which '·' occurs. Thus (B) is covered: by the rule for the quantifiers it is equivalent to a set of sentences in which '·' occurs flanked only by numerals, and those sentences receive their truth conditions via (A). Nevertheless, (A) together with the rules for the substitutional quantifiers do not suffice to *eliminate* '·' from all contexts: '·' is an indispensable part of the language. The same holds for substitutional quantification with respect to definite descriptions (the example of type (iii) at the beginning of this chapter). Russell's theory of descriptions is used to define the correlation which assigns the unquantified sentences of L1 their truth conditions, but the results is *not* a definition of the '(ix)' notation, not even a "contextual" definition. For, even a contextual definition is designed to provide eliminability. Its flexibility lies in the fact that the rules for elimination proceed sentence by sentence, rather than decreeing a single replacement for the defined notation on all occurrences. By contrast, my use of the theory of descriptions to provide truth conditions provides no elimination whatsoever, since the definite descriptions are wanted as substituends of the substitutional quantifiers. They are an indispensable part of the language.

In his recent discussion of the semantics of substitutional quantification, Saul Kripke gives a description of the addition of substitutional quantifiers to a fully referential base language which is similar to, but more restricted than the account of this chapter. Specifically, he requires that the contexts of the substitutional variables and their substituends be expressions already existing in the language. Thus methods (ii)–(iv) of passing from Li − 1 to Li described above are ruled out. The addition of (possibly) empty singular terms and substitutional variables for which they substitute to a fully referential base language is disallowed. Likewise, the addition of virtual class theory with substitutional variables taking class abstracta as substituends would be illegitimate. The chief impact of Kripke's policy is to foreswear the use of correlations like (C) which allow great freedom in assigning truth conditions to the unquantified sentences of Li via the sentences of $L0 \cup \ldots \cup Li - 1$. For, if both the substituends and their contexts are drawn from $L0 \cup \ldots \cup Li - 1$, then the unquantified sentences of Li will be sentences of $L0 \cup \ldots \cup Li - 1$ and hence already have their semantical interpretations.

Is there any rationale for Kripke's policy? I think not. Consider the example of type (iii), viz. the addition of substitutional variables with expressions of the form '(ix) ... x ...' as substituends (where '... x ...' is schematic for sentence of the base language open only in 'x'). Assuming the base language has the appropriate resources, we may form the sentence

(6) $(\exists x)_s \sim (x$ is a material object$)$.

This sentence is true iff one of its instances is; the set of its instances is recursive; the semantical interpretation of each instance is given in terms of Russell's theory of descriptions; is there any question that this sentence has received a *bona fide* semantical interpretation? Similarly, is there any question that the method of adding substitutionally quantified virtual class theory described above is adequate?

It may be objected that the loss of these examples is trivial since even within Kripke's framework, i.e. using only method (i), we can construct equivalent languages. In place of substitutional quantification with respect to terms of the form '(ix) ... x ...' we may use substitutional quantification with respect to open sentences of the base language in the context $\ulcorner (\exists x)(y)(\ldots y \ldots \equiv y = x \ .\& \ \phi x) \urcorner$ (where ϕ is a predicate of the base language). In place of (6) we will have

$(\exists F)_s \sim (\exists x)(y)(Fy \equiv y = x \ .\& \ x$ is a material object$)$,

which gathers for disjoint assertion precisely the sentences of the base language needed for (6). Substitutional quantification with respect to class abstracts in virtual class theory can be handled similarly. Thus methods (iii) and (iv) seem not to show any important strength beyond method (i).

There are two replies to this objection. First, the objection concedes the legitimacy of the other methods, and legitimacy is all that I have so far claimed. Indeed, constructing equivalent languages via method (i) may be taken as a demonstration that the languages constructed via (iii) and (iv) are given adequate semantical interpretation. In assessing method (i), Kripke says:

> I would have thought that any mathematical logician at this point would conclude that truth for L has been characterized uniquely. If someone asserts a [sentence of] L, we know precisely under what conditions his assertion would be true.[11]

If we can agree that this applies to (ii)–(iv) as well, I am satisfied. Second, in chapter VI we shall see a language of type (iv) which cannot be mimicked via method (i).

[11] Kripke, 1976, 333.

V

Application of the Criterion of Ontological Commitment to Languages with Substitutional Quantification

The criterion of ontological commitment is

    (C)   T is ontologically committed to a/F's iff T logically implies '$(\exists x)(x = a)$'/'$(\exists x)Fx$' and '$(\exists x)$' is understood objectually.

In order to apply (C) to languages with substitutional quantification we need to define logical implication for such languages. Quine once raised an objection against the possibility of reaching a reasonable definition,[1] but his objection was answered by Charles Parsons.[2] Since Parsons's reply to Quine affects our understanding of the semantics of languages with substitutional quantification, I will briefly portray the problem and its solution. In addition, there is an "irregularity" in the relation between the first order calculus and logical implication which calls for a decision concerning the definition of implication. This decision, as I will make it, has some significant consequences for the philosophy of logic, both in the context of languages with substitutional quantification and in general.

First, let's consider a simple question concerning the language of L of the last chapter: what is the ontological commitment of the sentence

    (1) $(\exists x)(x \in \{x: x \text{ is a horse}\})$?

We would like to say that (1) is committed to horses, but there is no obvious logical route from (1) to

    (2) $(\exists x)(x \text{ is a horse})$.

---

[1] Quine, 1973 [42], 105–10.
[2] Parsons, 1974, 6.

The connection between (1) and (2) is the correlation part of the semantics which provides that (2) gives the truth conditions of (1). Intuitively, this correlation should contribute to ontological commitment. It is on a par with the contribution of truth functions: if '$(\exists x)(x$ is green) & $(\exists x)(x$ is a mouse)' is committed to greens and mice via the commitments of '$(\exists x)(x$ is green)' and '$(\exists x)$ $(x$ is a mouse)', this is because the truth condition of the former sentence is given in terms of the latter sentences (in a particular way). Similarly, the commitment of (2) to horses accrues to (1) since the truth condition of (1) is given in terms of (2). It is easy enough to alter criterion (C) so as to provide for this intuition. All we need do is replace 'T logically implies' by 'T together with the equivalences formed from every pair of expressions explicitly correlated by the semantics logically implies'. Thus in addition to (1) we have

(3) $(x)(x \in \{x: \text{ is a horse}\} \equiv x \text{ is a horse})$

from which to deduce (2), and then the deduction is valid.

Even though this expedient answers to an obvious intuition, it may appear *ad hoc* as a modification of (C). Timothy McCarthy has suggested a way of understanding logical implication for languages with substitutional quantification which has the same result but requires no modification of (C), and has a clear intuitive basis as well. Since all sentences above level L0 have their truth conditions univocally based upon those of the sentences of L0, a semantical interpretation of L0 which determines the truth-values of its sentences does the same for all the sentences of the higher levels. Since L0 is a fully referential language, an interpretation of its sentences is the usual thing: a choice of denotata for singular terms, extensions for predicates, and range for the quantifiers. We may then define logical implication for the whole language—including the upper levels—as truth preservation in all interpretations of L0. Under this definition of logical implication, (1) directly implies (2), since the correlation guarantees that they will always have the same truth-value. Thus commitment flows up from L0 to the higher layers via the correlations and the substitutional semantics just as it should.

As an example of a language with substitutional quantification, L embodies a simplification which renders it atypical of the general case. The class abstracts replacing the substitutional variables of L1 were based on open sentences of L0 free only in 'x'. The result is that the instances of closed quantified sentences of L1 are closed with respect to variables of L0. This means that if a quantifier of L0 is attached to a closed sentence of L1, that quantifier is vacuous. This limitation simplifies the semantics greatly, as we shall see in the next paragraph, but it also seriously weakens the expressive power of L. We may simulate assertions about the set of apples in L1 if 'x is an apple' is a predicate of L0, since we will have the abstract '{x: x is an apple}' in L1. We may simulate assertions about the set of men each of whom loves some woman, if the predicate 'x is a man & $(\exists y)(y$ is a woman & x loves y)' is in L0, since we will have the abstract '{x: x is a man & $(\exists y)(y$ is a woman & x loves y)}' in L1. But suppose there is a woman for whom we have no particular specification, and we wish to simulate assertions about the set of all men who love her; for example, we may want to say that that class contains every member of Congress. The natural thing to say is this:

(4) $(\exists y)(y$ is a woman & $(x)(x$ is a member of Congress $\supset x \in \{x:$ x is a man & x loves y$\})$.

But this requires the use of an abstract which is open in variables other than 'x'. Now notice that if we do use such abstracts, then there will be quantified sentences of L1 which are closed, but have instances containing free variables of L0. For example,

(5) $(\exists a)(x)(x$ is a member of Congress $\supset x \in a)$

is closed in L1, but has

(6) $(x)(x$ is a member of Congress $\supset x \in \{x:$ x is a man & x loves y$\})$

as an instance, and (6) has 'y' free. This enables us to prefix quantifiers from L0 to closed sentences of L1 non-vacuously: the use of '$(\exists y)$' in

(7) $(\exists y)(\exists a)(x)(x$ is a member of Congress $\supset x \in a)$

is obviously non-vacuous in the light of (6).

By allowing abstracts open in variables other than 'x' as substituends of the substitutional variables of L1, we create a problem for the semantics of L1. (5) is a closed sentence of L1, and so we assume that its semantic interpretation should consist of a truth condition which will determine its truth-value. But if some of its instances are open, then they will not have truth conditions or a truth-value as their semantic interpretation; rather, they will be interpreted via *satisfaction* conditions. How then can the truth condition and truth value of (5) be defined in terms of its instances? A sentence of the form '$(\exists a)\phi a$' in L1 is true, we say, iff it has a true instance. If we define truth for the instances via the correlation to sentences in L0 and use Tarski semantics for L0, we will say that the instances are true iff they are satisfied by all sequences of objects. But this definition relies upon the fact that in Tarskian semantics a closed sentence is satisfied by all sequences of objects or by none. If a closed sentence of L1 has open instances, those instances will be satisfied by some sequences and not by others. Imagine then that a sentence of the form '$(\exists a)\phi a$' in L1 has no true closed instances, but has some open instances which are satisfied by some sequences and not by others. Then by ordinary lights we will say that the closed sentence also is satisfied by some sequences and not by others; how then shall we define truth for such a sentence?

Charles Parsons has answered this question as follows. In the ordinary Tarskian semantics as extended to substitutional quantification we define the truth conditions for quantified sentences of L1 via a rule for satisfaction, viz.

(8)   s satisfies '$(\exists a)\phi a$' iff some instance of 'ϕa' is satisfied by s

The difficulty arises if some of the instances of 'ϕa' have variables of L0 free; some sequences may satisfy such an instance and hence satisfy '$(\exists a)\phi a$' as well, while other sequences may satisfy neither. Parsons suggests we replace (8) with

(9)   s satisfies '$(\exists a)\phi a$' iff some instance of 'ϕa' is satisfied by an extension of s

where, given an instance of 'ϕa' with L0 variables $v_1, \ldots, v_n$ free, an extension of s is a sequence differing from s only with respect to those elements which will be assigned to $v_1, \ldots, v_n$.

The effect of (9) is to view every instance of 'ϕa' which has a variable of L0 free as if it was prefixed with existential quantifiers binding those variables. Thus *the instance will be treated as closed by the semantics* in the sense that it is either satisfied by all sequences or by none, and so the problem of the last paragraph disappears. Furthermore, as Parsons points out, this solves a problem which Quine has posed for the semantics and logic of L as liberalized in this chapter.

In his discussion of substitutional set theory, Quine tacitly assumed a context-dependent restriction on the substituends for the variables of L1, and then derived a problem for L1. The restriction which he used is this: a variable of L1 may be replaced in a context C by an abstract with a free variable v of L0 only if v is already free in C. Thus suppose 'Fx' abbreviates an open sentence of L0 with only 'x' free. Then the substitutional variable 'a' in

(10)   a is a unit sublcass of $\{x: Fx\}$

can be replaced only by closed abstracts, while in

(11)   a is a unit subclass of $\{x: Fx\}$ & $x=x$

it may be replaced by an abstract free in 'x'. The relation between Quine's restriction and (9) is the following. If we did not have (9), Quine's restriction would suffice to prevent the use of open abstracts as substituends from producing closed sentences which are satisfied by some sequences and not by others. For, we produced those sentences by taking closed quantified sentences of L1 and replacing their substitutional variables with open abstracts, and this the restriction would prevent. Now based upon his restriction, Quine develops the following problem. Consider the sentences

(12) $(\exists a)$(a is a unit subclass of $\{x: Fx\}$)
(13) $(\exists a)$(a is a unit subclass of $\{x: Fx\}$ & $x=x$).

Intuitively there are logically equivalent: (13) results from (12) by the addition of a logically true conjunct which should not make any difference. Nevertheless, (13) but not (12) follows logically from

(14) $\{y: y=x\}$ is a unit subclass of $\{x: Fx\}$ & $x=x$.

The reason is that the abstract '$\{y: y=x\}$' with its free variable 'x' can be substituted for 'a' only in (13) which has 'x' free, and not in (12) which is completely closed. Furthermore, continues Quine, it is possible to understand 'Fx' in (12) and (13) so that they differ with respect to satisfaction. Imagine that 'Fx' is a predicate which is true only of things which have no name in L0. Then (13) is satisfied by some sequences, while (12) is satisfied by none. (13) is satisfied by every sequence whose first member satisfies 'Fx', for, (13) has (14) as an instance, and (14) is satisfied by every such sequence. But (12) is false, for, every instance of (12) must have a closed abstract in place of 'a', and such an abstract will have to provide a name from L0 for its sole member and hence that object cannot satisfy 'Fx'. Thus (12) is satisfied by no sequences.

The answer to Quine's problem is clear from the foregoing. As Parsons has pointed out, if we drop Quine's restriction there are no untoward consequences for semantics and the problem dissolves. (Note also that the difference in truth-value between (12) and (13) rested upon the assumption that we have a predicate which is true only of nameless objects, and the existence of such predicates for a natural choice of L0 has yet to be shown.)[3]

I now turn to the concept of logical implication for languages with substitutional quantification, and in particular to the adequacy of the first order calculus (C). If we define implication semantically as suggested above, soundness follows immediately, but there is a problem with respect to completeness. For, if the class of substituends for 'a' is {a1, a2, ...}, substitutional semantics will count the following argument form valid:

(A) ϕa1,ϕa2,ϕa3, ...
Therefore, (a)ϕa.

The truth condition for the conclusion is simply that all of the premisses be true, hence any interpretation of the base language L0 which makes all the premisses true will make the conclusion true. However, in C an argument cannot make essential use of an infinite number of premisses: an argument is *defined* to have a finite number of premisses. On the usual—viz. referential—semantics this is no problem since the same holds true for implication: a sentence follows logically from an infinite set of sentences iff it follows from some finite subset. But for substitutional semantics this is not true, as is clear from (A): no finite subset of {ϕa1,ϕa2, ...} logically implies '(a)ϕa'. It appears, then, that C is incomplete with respect to substitutional validity.[4]

Furthermore, we cannot shrug off this problem as one which, since it affects only arguments with an infinite number of premisses, does not apply to arguments actually relied upon in proofs. The fact is that there are arguments with a finite number of premisses which are valid substitutionally and yet are not provable in C. For example, the validity of (A) in first order number theory is equivalent to omega-completeness, thus making possible a finite (semantically) complete

---

[3] Gila Sher has suggested that, if we allow a mixture of objectual quantification with respect to certain entities and substitutional quantification with respect to their names, we can formulate a predicate true only of nameless things as follows: (F)((y)(Fy ≡ x=y) ⊃ ~(∃a)Fa). (A simpler example is ~(∃a)(x = a).) The importance of such examples depends upon our need for such mixed quantification; I am not aware of any such need.

[4] Dunn and Belnap, 1968.

axiomatization. As an example of an argument with a finite number of premisses which is substitutionally valid and yet not provable in first order number theory, consider the Gödel sentence—abbreviated '(x)Gx'—and the axioms A1, . . . , An which suffice to logically imply all true closed unquantified sentences of number theory. (Usually A1, . . . , An are the axioms for successor, addition, and multiplication, without the induction axioms.) We know that '(x)Gx' is not provable from A1, . . . , An. We also know that 'Gx' contains only 'x' free and has no other variables. Thus if 'Gn' is the result of substituting the numeral 'n' for all free occurrence of 'x' in 'Gx', then 'Gn' is a closed unquantified sentence of number theory. Furthermore, we know that all those sentences follow from A1, . . . , An. But the argument

(G1)   G0,G1,G2, . . . ,
        Therefore (x)Gx

is of form (A) and so is valid (substitutionally). Thus by transitivity, the argument

(G2)   A1, . . . , An
        Therefore (x)Gx

is valid, and yet this is not provable in C.[5]

In order to overcome this problem, i.e., in order to restore the completeness of C, it has been suggested by some that substitutional validity be defined more narrowly so as to rule out (A) and with it (G1) and (G2).[6] The gist of the suggestion is that for validity we need not only truth preservation with respect to all the interpretations of the language in which the argument is expressed, but in addition truth preservation in all the interpretations of all extensions of the language. In particular, the truth preservation must not be affected by additions to the class of substituends for the substitutional quantifiers. Now it is clear that this redefinition of validity will do the trick. If we add a new

[5] See van Fraassen, 1971, 131: ". . . for any statement A, ⊩ in substitutional quantification languages iff ⊢ A in quantificational logic." How then can (G2) be substitutionally valid? Because a "substitutional quantification language" for van Fraasen contains an infinity of free variables which can be used to form instances of the substitutional variables. For such languages his theorem holds. However, the language of first order arithmetic with substitutional quantification does not have such free variables, and hence (G2) is valid. Thus van Fraasen's theorem is inapplicable to the languages we actually use (when substitutionally interpreted). In effect, he is assuming the use of a device like Leblanc's (see next footnote) to restore completeness to C.

[6] Leblanc, 1973, 6, and Kripke, 1976, 335–6.

constant 'c' to the language in which (A) is formulated, obviously (A) is no longer valid. The same goes for (G2): if we add 'c' then although all numeral instances of 'Gx' follow from A1, . . . , An, (x)Gx will not follow. But the trouble is that this is terribly *ad hoc*. We are confronted with the intuition mentioned in the beginning of this chapter: if truth is preserved by every interpretation of the primitives of the underlying level L0, and those interpretations suffice to determine truth values for all the sentences in the language, how can any more be needed for validity? Why should we consider what happens in other languages?

On the other hand, we have what appears to be a contrasting intuition expressed by Saul Kripke.[7] Adapting his thought to our context, the intuition is this. In referential semantics validity is truth preservation under all interpretations, and an interpretation assigns extensions to predicates, denotata to singular terms, *and a range for the variables*. How shall we understand the notion of an interpretation in substitutional semantics so that it will be parallel? Kripke answers: by viewing the sentences in the argument as abstracted from the language in which they are formulated and providing them with a linguistic setting whose elements can then be interpreted substitutionally. Thus part of the interpretation is the assignment of a substitution class to the substitutional variables in the argument. Just as in the setting of referential semantics we vary all factors which contribute to the truth-values of the sentence of the argument (except the interpretation of the logical constants), so should we vary all such factors in the setting of substitutional semantics. Just as the range of the variables is such a factor in the referential setting, so the substitution class for the variables is such a factor in the substitutional setting. In the light of this intuition the argument (G1) appears invalid. We thought it was valid because we illicitly fixed the substitution class of the quantifier '(x)'.

Against Kripke it may be urged that the analogy between substitutionally interpreted quantifiers and objectually interpreted quantifiers is not that close; in many ways the former are more similar to infinitary extensions of conjunction and disjunction. We do not require truth functions to vary from interpretation to interpretation and so we should not vary substitutional quantifiers either.

For his part, Kripke could argue that whether or not an argument is valid ought to be decided by the logical forms of the sentences of the

[7] Kripke, 1976, 335–6.

argument. To regard (G1) as valid violates this rule, since if we imbed
(G1) in a language in which the substitution class for 'x' contains an
expression not identical to any of 0,1,2, . . . this will not be the case.
But, it seems to me that this argument only carries weight if one is in
the grip of a strongly componential semantics in which one can give a
complete account of the semantics of a particular sentence in
abstraction from the rest of the language of which it is a part. The
formal aspects of that semantics will determine the sentence's logical
form, and so validity as well is language independent in this sense. But
for languages with substitutional quantification we do not have
strongly componential semantics: the semantic interpretation of a
sentence often requires linking it to other sentences of the language.
There is no reason why formal aspects of this linkage cannot play a
role in determining the logical relations among sentences. It is in this
sense that (A) is a valid argument form and (G1), being an argument
of that form, is valid.

Kripke's intuition may derive some strength (illicitly) from a misunderstanding of argument form (A) and how it is to be applied. We
are imagining a1,a2,a3, . . . to be all the substituends of the quantifier
'(a)'. Now is (A) to be understood like this:

(A) ϕa1,ϕa2,ϕa3, . . . , and a1,a2,a3, . . . are all the substituends of
      '(a)'
      Therefore (a)ϕa

or like this:

(A*) ϕa1,ϕa2,ϕa3, . . .
       Therefore (a)ϕa?

In other words, is the fact that a1,a2,a3, . . . exhaust all the substituends for '(a)' part of the description of the form of argument or
not? If not, then it is easy to see why arguments such as (G1) are not
thought valid. They are being classified as instances of form (A*) and
there are other arguments of form (A*) which are clearly invalid: argument G1 in a language with individual constants other than 0,1,2, . . .
is an example. But if the exhaustiveness of the substituends is taken
as part of the description of the argument, i.e. if the form is understood as (A) of this paragraph, then that is obviously no longer the
case: there are not obviously invalid instances of (A). The only
remaining question then is this: is there some reason not to allow
reference to the exhaustiveness of the substituends in describing a form

of argument? I don't think so. The only guideline we have for describing forms of argument is that the descriptions be really formal, that no features of the particular vocabulary or subject matter of the argument be cited. Though this characterization is somewhat vague, (A) seems safely formal. What is different about (A) is that it appeals to a formal feature of the relation between the premises of an argument and the rest of the language of which it is a part, but the feature is not the less formal for that. I conclude that there is ample justification for rejecting Kripke's intuition and the suggested reformulation of substitutional validity. Of course this is not to say that I have proved the approach of Kripke *et al.* to be incorrect, but only that the definition of validity adopted here represents a different approach which is also viable.

If our formal logic is incomplete (and incompleteable in principle) with respect to substitutional validity and the latter is incorporated into the criterion (C), we must acknowledge that our theories may have ontological commitments which we can in principle never know. For, there may be ontological commitments due to logical implications for which there are no *recognizably* valid arguments. I am not frightened by this prospect. It is no argument against a theory of logic that it does not enable us to become omniscient. Even as referentially interpreted the first order calculus is undecidable, and so we cannot know in all cases whether a given argument is valid. It is true that completeness would enable us to say that all valid arguments are findable in principle, but when we know in advance that due to lack of resources an infinite number of them will in fact go undiscovered, my interest in principles wanes. There are those who feel that logic has some inherent right to be complete and that any modification of this feature *ipso facto* enters some non-logical sphere.[8] I find this point of view without rationale. The correlation of syntactic and semantic properties which we find in *C* as referentially interpreted I view as overwhelmingly surprising—a little piece of Leibnizian predetermination actually coming to life! We should not expect it to continue. And even there one might ask: why the focus on completeness, with respect to which it does work out, rather than on decidability where it doesn't?[9]

[8] Quine, 1973 [43], 90–1.
[9] Boolos, 1975, 523.

Part II

Application

VI

Substitutional Arithmetic

(0) Introduction

Enquiry into the foundations of mathematics has a three-fold responsibility: epistemology—i.e., an account of mathematical knowledge; metaphysics—an account of that portion of reality with which mathematics deals; and semantics—a theory of meaning for the language of mathematics. The three interlock in an obvious way: semantics must link mathematical language to that portion of reality whose nature is disclosed in mathematical knowledge. Constraints on proposed foundations for mathematics may be discovered by exploring the needs of each component. If those needs are not consistent, then it will be very difficult to envision the possibility of any acceptable foundations for mathematics. Paul Benaceraff believes that they are not consistent and hence that it is extremely doubtful that there can be any acceptable account of mathematics.[1] Here is a brief sketch of his reasons.

One traditional view of mathematics is realism—the "window view" as I shall call it. One portion of reality is an abstract realm of mathematical entities—numbers, functions, sets, and so on. Mathematics is the study of these entities. Through its methods of proof we gain knowledge of their properties and relations. The semantics for the language of mathematics which this view requires is the usual referential account of singular terms, predicates, and quantifiers which link those expressions to the domain of mathematical entities. Given the common understanding of abstract objects as non-spatiotemporal, the window view violates the following constraint on epistemology: knowledge of objects must be mediated by causal interaction with those objects. Since there are no causal relations with abstracta, if this constraint holds the window view is out.

The only alternative to the window view is to radically reinterpret the language of mathematics, as is done by the intuitionists, for

[1] Benaceraff, 1973.

example. Mathematical sentences are interpreted as assertions about the (actual or possible) existence of constructions or proofs. While such an account may ease the formulation of mathematical epistemology, it violates what Benacerraf takes to be a crucial constraint of semantics, viz. that an account of mathematical language must integrate directly into our overall semantics so that it be clear that the account is an account of *truth* and not just some (possibly coextensive) property. The radical reinterpretation of mathematical language which alternatives to the window view require violate this constraint according to Benaceraff.

In sum, Benaceraff discerns the following dilemma: either you have the window view with an acceptable semantics for mathematical language, but mathematical knowledge is impossible; or you have some kind of "verificationist" view which makes mathematical knowledge possible, but which cannot provide a *bona fide* theory of truth for mathematical language. In my opinion, Benaceraff goes wrong on two counts. First, the window view is not only a disaster for epistemology; it is equally a disaster for semantics. Benaceraff stresses two features of general semantics: (i) "the semantical apparatus of mathematics [must] be seen as part and parcel of that of the natural language in which it is done"—which means that if a mathematical sentence and a non-mathematical sentence are clearly parallel in structure then they should receive the same logical form, and (ii) the theory of truth for a language "... must proceed through reference and satisfaction and, furthermore, must be supplemented with an account of reference itself".[2] I agree that the standard semantics for mathematics fits (i), but the inevitability of the window view on this semantics seems to jeopardize (ii). For, it is hard to envisage an *account* of reference with respect to mathematical objects—and for reasons very close to those which make us sceptical concerning our knowledge of those objects. Just as causality has come to play a large role in the analysis of knowledge, and thus our lack of causal interaction with mathematical objects hamstrings our account of how we know them, so causality looms large in attempts to account for various features of reference, and thus we will be at a loss to explain how we can refer to those objects. Thus I see the window view as problematic not only for epistemology, but also for semantics.[3]

[2] Benaceraff, 1973, 677.
[3] Jubien, 1977.

Second, Benaceraff has overlooked another alternative in addition to a window view and a verificationist view: an interpretation of the language of mathematics as part of a language with substitutional quantification. This interpretation will escape Benaceraff's dilemma. By incurring no commitment to mathematical objects, it avoids the epistemological problems of the window view. And, although the traditional Tarski semantics for mathematical language is not retained, interpreting that language as an upper level of a language with substitutional quantification cannot be attacked as a failure to provide a theory of truth. Furthermore, it is not clear that my account will deviate from the specific requirement which Benaceraff places on a theory of truth, namely that sentences with clearly parallel structure be given the same logical form. For if we limit our vision to the level in which mathematical sentences appear, their form will be identical with that prescribed by the traditional account. The only change on that level will be to interpret the quantifiers substitutionally, and thus postpone the question of ontological commitment to the interpretation of the unquantified sentences of that level. The account of their truth conditions will differ radically from the tradition: they will be assigned truth conditions via a correlation to sentences in a language which has no mathematical vocabulary whatsoever. Nevertheless, since at the bottom of the partition is a language L0 which is fully referential, we will have explained the truth conditions of the sentences of mathematics in terms of an account of how those sentences connect with the world. Thus such an account has every right to claim the title of a theory of truth for the language of mathematics.

The proposed semantics for the language of mathematics has a strong salutary effect upon the epistemological and metaphysical responsibilities of foundations. The axioms and theorems of mathematics will be logically true in the very narrow sense of infinite bundles of first order tautologies of the referential language L0. While this in itself does not provide a mathematical epistemology, it reduces the problem of providing one to the corresponding problem for first order logic. As for metaphysics, we will be rid of a crucial difficulty engendered by the window view. If the window view is true, then the physical world in which we live and strive to understand and control is utterly different and divorced from the realm about which mathematics gives us knowledge. It is then a mystery how such knowledge can be of service to us. How can information concerning such eternal abstracta as numbers and functions help us build bridges or discover the chemical composition of the stars? On my account the theorems of "pure" mathematics will be logical truths relating those sentences of L0 which express *mathematical applications*. Thus pure mathematics can be seen as part of the logic of those applications.

The rest of this chapter will present the substitutional semantics for the language of first order arithmetic. The plan of the chapter is as follows. In section (1) the syntax and semantics of substitutional first order arithmetic are presented. In section (2) the truth-values thus accorded to the sentences of arithmetic are compared to the standard distribution of truth-values; divergences are noted and justified. Section (3) considers objections. Section (4) presents a modified axiomatization for number theory and section (5) examines the impact of the new semantics on the use of definition in number theory. Section (6) closes the chapter with a comparison between my account of arithmetic and older forms of Logicism.

(1) Syntax and Semantics for Substitutional Arithmetic

We start with a language L0 which is wholly referential, i.e., whose primitive vocabulary consists of predicates, singular terms, truth-functional connectives, quantifiers, and identity, all interpreted referentially. Only one restriction is placed on L0: it contains no mathematical vocabulary whatsoever. Nevertheless, it is well known that since L0 contains quantification and identity, it does have the resources to form sentences which I shall call *attributions of multiplicity*, namely sentences asserting 'there are exactly n things such that ——.' In multiplicity attributions I see the basic application of arithmetic to the physical world. Accordingly, those sentences of L0 will be the link between the world and the sentences of pure arithmetic.

To form L1 we introduce three new groups of expressions: (i) substitutional variables 'F', 'G', ... and their quantifiers which take open sentences of L0 as their substituends; (ii) substitutional variables 'm', 'n', 'r', ... and their quantifiers which take formal numerals (i.e., 0, 0', 0'', ...) as their substituends; and (iii) all instances of the schema '∃!ABC' where 'A' is replaced by a variable of group (ii) or a formal numeral, 'B' by a variable of L0, and 'C' by either a substitutional variable of (i) or an open sentence of L0. I will first explain the intent behind the new sentences of L1 and then give its precise semantics.

The expressions of group (iii) are intended to be understood as equivalent to multiplicity attributions. Thus '∃!0'x(x is bald)' can be read: there is exactly one thing x such that x is bald, or more simply, there is exactly one bald thing. Truth conditions for the sentences in this group will be given via a correlation to the multiplicity attributions of L0. Now there is no restriction upon the open sentences which can occur in the 'C' slot. Thus we will have to make sense of sentences like '∃!0′x(y is bald)' and '∃!0′x(x is taller than y)', since we cannot expect that the free variables of the open sentence will be exactly the free variable of the exclamation operator. If the open sentence does not have the operator variable free at all, then the whole will be understood to assert the existence of a certain number of entities without any condition, conjoined with the open sentence—the whole being an open sentence. Thus '∃!0′x(y is bald)' will be interpreted as saying: there is exactly one thing, and y is bald. If the open sentence has the operator variable free and others in addition, it will be interpreted as asserting the existence of a certain numbers of entities standing in the relation of the open sentence to unspecified entities which are the values of the other free variables. Thus '∃!0′x(x is taller than y)' will be interpreted as saying: there is exactly one thing which is taller than y. The flexibility of using open sentences free in variables other than the operator variable is very important since attributions of multiplicity are often made relationally, e.g., if someone is the next-to-tallest then there is someone than whom exactly one person is taller, i.e., (∃y)∃!0′x(x is taller than y).

The quantifiers and variables of group (i) have the characteristic effect of substitutional quantification: they enable us to gather up infinities of sentences for joint assertion without ascending to the meta-language or using semantic terms. Thus they increase the expressive power of L0 directly—consider defining 'x = y' as '(F)(Fx ≡ Fy)' for example. But our concern will be with the way in which they interact with the exclamation expressions. When the 'C' slot of the exclamation schema is occupied by a variable of L1, we gain the ability to assert infinities of multiplicity attributions, and certain of these will be used directly to give the truth conditions of the sentences of arithmetic. For example, consider

(1)   (F)(G)((∃!0′xF & ∃!0″xG & ~(∃x)(F & G))

⊃ ∃!0‴x(F ∨ G)),

i.e., if there is exactly one F, exactly two G's, and nothing is both F and G, then there are exactly three F-or-G's. (1) expresses a certain relation between multiplicity attributions for any pair of open sentences, and in fact characterizes the use of addition in relation to them. This relation will be exploited below. As with the exclamation expressions we must take care concerning open sentences which have free variables other than those which will be captured by the context of the variable. If the 'F' in '(F)($\exists$x)F' is replaced by 'x is bald' well and good; but if it is replaced by 'y is bald' or 'x is taller than y' then the originally closed sentence '(F)($\exists$x)F' has open instances, and this requires care in formulating the truth definition. The situation is exactly parallel to that of virtual set theory whose treatment by Charles Parsons was outlined in chapter V; the same method will be used here.

The quantifiers and variables of group (ii) enable us to express general relations among multiplicity attributions, but the generality concerns the multiplicity attributed, not the open sentences to which it is attributed. Thus we may assert with confidence that ($\exists$n)$\exists$!nx(x is bald) even if we don't know exactly how many baldies there are. More important is the fact that with the resources of group (ii) we can express relations between the multiplicities of open sentences whose exact count is unknown. That there are exactly as many A's as B's is expressed by '($\exists$n)($\exists$!nxA & $\exists$!nxB)', and once we have arithmetic operations available we can express 'there are more A's and B's' by '($\exists$m)($\exists$n)($\exists$!mxA & $\exists$!nxB & m is greater than n)'. It is obviously of great importance for the applicability of pure arithmetic to attributions of multiplicity that these quantifiers be available in L1.

Now the formal semantics for L1. The exclamation sentences which have open sentences of L0 in the 'C' slot are assigned truth conditions via the following correlation with multiplicity attributions of L0:

(R1)   If S is an open sentence of L0, v is a variable of L0, and a is a formal numeral, then the truth condition of $\ulcorner\exists$!0vS$\urcorner$ is $\ulcorner\sim(\exists$v)S$\urcorner$, and the truth condition of $\ulcorner\exists$!a′vS$\urcorner$ is $\ulcorner(\exists$u)(S^v/u & $\exists$!a(S & v$\neq$u))$\urcorner$, where u is the first variable of L0 (under a suitable ordering) not occurring in S, and S^v/u is the result of substituting u for all free occurrences of v in S.

Used recursively, (R1) associates with exclamation sentences the multiplicity attributions of L0 which express their intuitive content. For example, via (R1) the truth condition of '$\exists$!0″x(x is bald)' is

($\exists$y) (y is bald & ($\exists$z)(z is bald & y$\neq$z & $\sim(\exists$x) (x is bald
    & x$\neq$y & x$\neq$z))),

which expresses 'there are exactly two bald things'. It is important to notice that (R1) is *only* a rule which associates recursively the exclamation sentences of L1 with their truth conditions in L0. It cannot be regarded as a definition of the exclamation notation, not even as a contextual definition, since that notation forms an ineliminable context for the substitutional quantifiers of L1. The situation here is parallel to that of the definite description operator in chapter IV.

The new quantifiers of group (i) are substitutional. Nevertheless, we cannot simply accord them the usual substitutional interpretation, viz. '$(\exists F)\phi$' is true iff some substitution instance of 'ϕ' is true, because we allow open sentences to replace 'F' in such a way as to give *open* instances to a sentence of L1 which is closed. If we want the closed sentences of L1 to have truth-values, we must make sure that they are each satisfied by all or no sequences. This is accomplished by using Parsons's method:

(R2) $\ulcorner(\exists F)\phi\urcorner$ is satisfied by s iff some instance of ϕ is satisfied by some extension of s.

Although the formulation of the truth conditions for the sentences of arithmetic does not trade on the ability of (R2) to provide truth-values in spite of open instances of closed sentences, the logic of L1 relies upon it heavily, and so it is important for the proof of the logical truth of the axioms of arithmetic. Similarly, we need a satisfaction rule and not a truth rule for the quantifiers of group (ii), not because they generate closed sentences with open instances, but rather because when they combine with quantifiers of group (i) they will be attached to open sentences. For example, among the instances of '$(\exists F)(\exists n)\exists!nxF$' we have '$(\exists n)\exists!nx(y$ is bald)', and the semantical interpretation of the numeral quantifier must be expressed in terms of satisfaction in order to apply to the latter. However, since the instances of a group (ii) quantification cannot have any free variables which were not present in the quantification itself, we do not need to make Parsons' appeal to the extension of a sequence. So the rule is:

(R3) $\ulcorner(\exists n)\phi\urcorner$ is satisfied by s iff s satisfies some instance of ϕ.

We now pass to the language of first order arithmetic which occupies level L2 and which I shall call *AL0* (for *arithmetic of L0*). The primitive vocabulary of AL0 consists of the formal numerals and the variables and quantifiers of group (ii) of L1, and in addition the dyadic predicate symbol '=' and the triadic predicate letters 'S' and 'P'. The quantifiers will be interpreted substitutionally via the rule

(Q) $\ulcorner(\exists n)\phi\urcorner$ is true iff some substitution instance of ϕ (i.e. the result of uniformly substituting a numeral for 'n' in ϕ) is true.

Notice that we need not appeal to Parsons's method here since the contexts in which the variables of AL0 appear are not those in which there are any variables of L0 or L1, hence there is no question of having an open instance of a closed sentence of AL0. Instances of closed sentences of AL0 may be correlated to sentences of L1 which *latter* have open instances, but that is handled by (R2).

The heart of the semantics of AL0 is the assignment of truth conditions to the unquantified sentences of AL0. These are of three kinds: $\ulcorner a = b\urcorner$, $\ulcorner Sabc\urcorner$, and $\ulcorner Pabc\urcorner$, where a, b, and c are numerals. The guiding principle behind the assignment—which will be in the form of a correlation with sentences of L1—is that the application of arithmetic, and in particular of the numerals, is in the context of multiplicity attributions. First the rule for $\ulcorner a = b\urcorner$:

(=) $\ulcorner a = b\urcorner$ is true iff $\ulcorner(F)(\exists!axF \equiv \exists!bxF)\urcorner$ is true.

What (=) says is that $\ulcorner a = b\urcorner$ is true iff a and b may be substituted for one another in all exclamation sentences without altering truth-value. This means that a and b are multiplicity equivalent: they "count" exactly the same predicates. From the point of view of applications as here conceived, that means that there is no difference of any account between them. Nevertheless, it must be clearly understood that '=' is not being used as the sign of identity in so far as one conceives of identity as a logical notion. Rather '=' expresses a kind of indiscernability (or better: interchangeability – there are no entities to apply (in)discernability to in this context) with respect (ultimately) to *L0*'s multiplicity attributions. Why then do I use the traditional symbol for identity? Because it follows from (=) that $\ulcorner a = b\urcorner$ licenses the substitution of a for b *salva veritate* throughout the language of AL0; the traditional axioms of identity are all true with respect to '=' under the interpretation given by (=). Thus '=' functions formally as identity in AL0, even though semantically it is understood quite differently.

Next comes addition. The most common application of addition to multiplicity attributions is to relate them conditionally as follows. '4 + 2 = 6' tells us that if there are (exactly) 4 of these and 2 of those, and nothing is both one of these and one of those, then there are

6 of these and those together. In general, the truth condition for a sentence $\ulcorner Sabc \urcorner$ is given by:

(S) $\ulcorner Sabc \urcorner$ is true iff $\ulcorner (F)(G)((\exists!axF \ \& \ \exists!bxG \ \& \ \sim(\exists x)(F \ \& \ G))$ $\supset \exists!cx(F \lor G)) \urcorner$ is true.

The instances of the right side of (S) are precisely the sentences of L1 which, when interpreted via (R1), express the conditional relationship between multiplicity attributions of L0 which typifies the application of addition.

Multiplication will be treated recursively in terms of addition in the standard manner, viz.

(P) $\ulcorner P0b\alpha \urcorner$ is true iff $\ulcorner S00\alpha \urcorner$ is true, and $\ulcorner Pa'b\alpha \urcorner$ is true iff $\ulcorner (\exists\beta)(Pab\beta \ \& \ S\beta b\alpha) \urcorner$ is true.

The recursive use of (P) requires us to take α as either a numeral or a variable of AL0; in the latter case β is the first variable after α. (P) interprets multiplication as repeated addition; e.g. $P0''0''0''''$ has as its truth condition

$(\exists m)((\exists n)(P00''n \ \& \ Sn0''m) \ \& \ Sm0''0'''')$

which says that something ('n') is the product of 0 and $0''$, and when added to $0''$ gives something else ('m'), and the latter, when added to $0''$ gives $0''''$. But the first clause of (P) makes it clear that to require that something be the product of 0 and anything is to require that the former be 0, and so the relation between 'm' and 'n' is simply that 0 plus $0''$ is m, and m plus $0''$ is $0''''$. Note that (P) is an "inductive definition" which (together with the interpretation of the quantifiers) supplies truth conditions for all sentences in which 'P' appears in terms of sentences which already have truth conditions (cf. chapter IV). Interpreting multiplication as repeated addition accords with the typical application of multiplication which is to find the total of a number of equinumerous groups.

It is important to see that these truth conditions allow for the application of arithmetic to relational, as well as absolute, multiplicity attributions. Not only does (S) enable us to conclude that there are exactly four apples or oranges from the information that there are exactly two apples and exactly two oranges; it also enables us to conclude that there is a mountain which has been climbed by exactly four men or women from the information that there is a mountain which has been climbed by exactly two men and exactly two women. (S) can do this because its quantifiers '(F)' and '(G)' allow open sentences as substituends; thus

$$\exists!0''x(x \text{ is a man \& } x \text{ climbed } y) \text{ \& } \exists!0''x(x \text{ is a woman \& } x$$
$$\text{climbed } y) \text{ \& } \sim(\exists x)(x \text{ is a man \& } x \text{ is a woman \& } x \text{ climbed } y). \supset$$
$$\exists!0''''x((x \text{ is a man \& } x \text{ climbed } y) \lor (x \text{ is a woman \& } x \text{ climbed } y))$$

is an instance of (S) and enables us to make the described transition.

Before we evaluate this assignment of truth conditions, I wish to note how it illustrates the themes of chapter IV. First, notice the particular structure of the language L0 ∪ L1 ∪ AL0. L0 is extended to L1 by adding two forms of substitutional quantification, one with respect to substituends which are expressions of L0 (open sentences) and one with respect to newly introduced substituends (formal numerals). We reach AL0 by extending the contexts available to the second type of substitutional quantification in L1: all of the new vocabulary of AL0 is used solely to provide more contexts for the formal numerals and their substitutional variables. Second, Davidson's definition of semantic primitive does not apply to the semantics for AL0 since according to that definition none of the following is a semantic primitive: 0,0′,0″, . . . , 'S'. The numerals are not primitive since e.g., the sentences '(n)(n = n)', '(n)Snnn' and '(n)Pnnn' contain no numerals, and yet they require all of the semantical rules for their interpretation, and those rules suffice to interpret all sentences containing numerals; hence the rules for sentences *not* containing numerals also provide for all the sentences which do contain numerals. Likewise for 'S': since in order to interpret '(n)Pnnn' we need both (P) and (S), the rules needed for a sentence *not* involving 'S' suffice to interpret all the sentences which do involve 'S', hence 'S' is not primitive. It is clear that the semantics for AL0 is not strongly componential. It is very hard to ascribe to the numerals anything which resembles a traditional semantical role. Their job is to recursively indicate a context-dependent structure of quantification and identity which is characteristic of multiplicity assertions; I don't think anything more helpful can be said about them. 'S' indicates a certain complex context into which the numerals are plugged so that they can trigger the right combination of quantifiers and identity for each of the instances on the right side of (S). And the role of 'P' cannot be usefully described in prose; the recursion (P) does it best. The role of the prime should also be noted. It is of course not a function symbol; it is a syntactical part of the individual constants of

AL0 and is recognized as such in so far as we tolerate such sentences as '(m)(n)(m′=n′ ⊃ m=n)'. The intelligibility of this sentence despite the fact that the prime has no semantical interpretation at all in AL0 typifies the usefulness of substitutional quantification. It is because of the complexity of cases like this (and this is, after all, rather elementary) that I think there can be no useful characterization of the *form* which assignments of truth conditions can take. Finally, it is clear that an account of the semantics of a sentence such as '(n)(0 ≠ n′)' will require a description of its truth conditions on all three levels; a one-line schema cannot do the job.

With respect to the comparison to Kripke's treatment of sub-stitutional quantification, I pointed out above that the exclamation expressions of L1 are not defined by (R1) and indeed cannot be defined if the quantifiers of L1 are to be meaningful. They are new expressions emerging at L1; L1 does not arise from L0 solely by the addition of substitutional quantifiers whose substitution classes are expressions of L0. Thus the step from L0 to L1 would not be sanctioned by Kripke, and yet it is obviously semantically legitimate, and necessary for the understanding of AL0. The same is true of AL0 itself, since '=', 'S', and 'P' are not expressions of L1. Likewise, it is hard to see how an equivalent language could be constructed within the bounds of method (i) of chapter IV. The sentence '(∃n)∃!nx(x is bald)' gathers together the following sentences for disjoint assertion:

∼(∃x)(x is bald)
(∃y)(y is bald & ∼(∃x)(x is bald & x≠y))
(∃y)(y is bald & (∃z)(z is bald & y≠z & ∼(∃x)(x is bald & x≠y & x≠z)))
. . .

If we were required to introduce substitutional variables whose sub-stituends are expressions of L0, how would we accomplish this?

(2) Truth Conditions for Applied Arithmetic

We will start the evaluation of the assignment of truth conditions to the sentences of AL0 by comparing the truth-*values* of those sentences under that assignment with their truth-values in the standard model (their *standard* truth-values). The facts may be summarized as follows: (i) all standardly true atomic sentences of AL0 are true on my assignment—in fact, *logically* true; (ii) some standardly false atomic sentences of AL0 *may be true* on my assignment, and the reason they have whatever truth-value they have is *non-mathematical*; and (iii) some non-atomic sentences of AL0 which are standardly true may be *false* on my assignment, and the reason they have whatever truth-value they have is also non-mathematical. (i) is obviously a happy result; (ii) and (iii) must be explained. Some of the sentences included in (iii) are accepted *axioms* of first order arithmetic, hence the explanation must show why those axioms should not be accepted. But first let's see that (i)–(iii) are true.

A standardly true sentence $\ulcorner a = b \urcorner$ is one in which a and b are the same numeral, and hence one whose truth condition via (=) is $\ulcorner (F)(\exists!axF \equiv \exists!axF) \urcorner$. Such a sentence of L1 is interpreted by (R2) to be an infinite bundle of sentences of L0 each of which is of the form '$\phi \equiv \phi$'. Hence when we trace a standardly true sentence $\ulcorner a = b \urcorner$ to its ultimate truth conditions, we find an infinite bundle of sentences in L0 which are logically true in the strictest sense—the sense of standard first order logic. Although I have no proof for it, it seems to me that this entitles the former to the title of logical truth as well. After all, we allow finite conjunctions of logically true sentences the title of logical truth; can the passage to infinity so change the semantics of epistemological or metaphysical status of a sentence as to make this title inappropriate? I think not, especially in a case like ours where the relation between the sentence and its infinite bundle of logical truths is ideal in all respects: the infinite bundle is recursive; the relation between each sentence $\ulcorner a = b \urcorner$ and its bundle is decidable; we can recursively produce all the proofs for logical truth of the elements of the bundle; etc. Thus I will use the term "logically true" to include such cases from now on without explicit qualification.

A standardly true sentence $\ulcorner Sabc \urcorner$ is also logically true. This can be seen by example. Consider $S0'0''0'''$. Its truth condition is

(2) $(F)(G)((\exists!0'xF \ \& \ \exists!0''xG \ \& \ {\sim}(\exists x)(F \ \& \ G))$
      $\supset \exists!0'''x(F \lor G)).$

If we let 'A' and 'B' abbreviate open sentences of L0, the following is a representative instance of (2):

(3) $(\exists!0'xA \ \& \ \exists!0''xB \ \& \ {\sim}(\exists x)(A \ \& \ B)) \supset \exists!0'''x(A \lor B).$

We get the truth condition for (3) via (R1); somewhat simplified, it is:

(4) $((\exists x)(y)(Ay \equiv y{=}x) \ \& \ (\exists x)(\exists y)(z)((Bz \equiv (z{=}x \lor z{=}y)) \ \&$

$\sim(\exists x)(A \,\&\, B)) \supset (\exists x)(\exists y)(\exists z)(w)((Aw \vee Bw)$

$\equiv (w{=}x \vee w{=}y \vee w{=}z)).$

It is obvious that (4) is a first order logically true sentence of L0. So $S0'0''0'''$ has (2) as its truth condition, which in turn has an infinity of sentences on a par with (3) as its truth condition, and the truth conditions of the latter sentences are given by sentences on a par with (4): $S0'0''0'''$ has as its ultimate truth condition an infinity of sentences like (4), and since the latter are all logically true, so is the former.

Finally, a standardly true sentence $\ulcorner Pabc \urcorner$ is also logically true. Taking as an example $P0''0''0''''$, we get the truth condition

(5) $(\exists m)((\exists n)(P00''n \,\&\, Sn0''m) \,\&\, Sm0''0'''')$.

(5) is logically true by our lights if one of its instances is, since the truth condition for (5) via (R2) is simply that one of its instances be true. Consider the instance

(6) $P00''0 \,\&\, S00''0'' \,\&\, S0''0''0''''$.

We get a truth condition wholly in terms of 'S' if we apply (P) to the first conjunct:

(7) $S000 \,\&\, S00''0'' \,\&\, S0''0''0''''$.

All of the conjuncts of (7) are standardly true, so they are all logically true, and so (7), (6), (5) are finally $P0''0''0''''$ are all logically true. So (i) is verified.

To illustrate (ii)—that some standardly false unquantified sentences of AL0 may be true under my assignment of truth conditions, and whatever truth-value they have is due to non-mathematical factors—consider

(8) $0''' = 0''''$.

(8) is standardly false. Its truth condition via ($=$) is

(9) $(F)(\exists!0'''xF \equiv \exists!0''''xF)$.

Now $\exists!0'''xF$ and $\exists!0''''xF$ are logically incompatible, but they are not *contradictories*, they are *contraries*. Thus it is logically possible for them both to be false. And it easy to describe a situation in which they will both be false no matter what open sentence of L0 goes in for 'F'—i.e., a situation in which all instances of (9) will be *true*—namely, when there are less than three entities in the universe. For in such a universe it will always be false to say that there are exactly three so-and-sos, and also always false to say that there are exactly four so-and-sos. In general, any sentence $\ulcorner a = b \urcorner$ will be true if the universe contains less than min(a,b) members; thus many sentences of that form which are standardly false will be true in such a universe. Now we don't know how big our universe is. It might even be infinite; and it is even conceivable that there might be *a priori* reasons for holding that it is infinite. But it seems clear that whatever those reasons may be, they are non-mathematical, and thus my truth conditions for these sentences make their truth dependent upon non-mathematical factors. Thus *either* my assignment of truth conditions results in a non-standard distribution of truth-values to the (unquantified) sentences of AL0, *or* it results in the standard distribution, but this result is due to non-mathematical factors.

It might be thought that the predicate quantifier in (9) makes its truth value not dependent solely on the size of the universe; the stock of predicates in L0 ought to also play a role. If the universe is not large enough then (9) will certainly be true, but even if the universe if large enough, we need a substituend for 'F' to falsify (9). Does the availability of such a substituend depend upon the expressive power of L0? No, it does not. If we make use of relational multiplicity we can construct a predicate with any multiplicity up to (and including) the cardinality of the universe from the *purely logical* resources of L0, as follows: for any $n \leqslant \overline{\overline{U}}$ it is true that

$$(\exists x_1) \ldots (\exists x_n)\exists!nx(x=x_1 \vee \ldots \vee x=x_n).$$

Thus (9) is guaranteed a false instance if the universe is large enough, and thus the problem concerning sentences like (9) is solely a problem concerning the size of the universe.

As a second illustration, consider

(10)   S0′′′0″0′′′′′′.

Its truth condition is

(11) $(F)(G)((\exists!0′′′xF \ \& \ \exists!0″xG \ \& \ \sim(\exists x)(F \ \& \ G)))$
         $\supset (\exists!0′′′′′′x(F \vee G))$.

As a universally quantified conditional, (11) will be true (in spite of the fact that S0′′′0″0′′′′′′ is standardly false) if all instances of the antecedent are false. The antecedent of (11) says that there are three so-and-sos, two such-and-suches, and nothing is a so-and-so and such-

and-such: if the universe has less than five things in it, this will always be false and consequently (11) will be true—and any replacement for the consequent of (11) will preserve this fact. Thus in a less than five-membered universe ⌜S0′′′0′′a⌝ is true for all a. In general, if the universe has fewer members than what we call the sum of a and b, ⌜Sabc⌝ will be true for all c. On the other hand, if the universe if large enough, there will always be a false instance of (11). Such an instance is constructed using relational multiplicity, as follows: asuming there are at least five members of the universe, take 'x=x_1 ∨ x=x_2 ∨ x=x_3' as 'F', and 'x=x_4 ∨ x=x_5' as 'G'. The false instance of (11) is:

$$∃!0′′′x(x=x_1 ∨ x=x_2 ∨ x=x_3) \ \& \ ∃!0′′x(x=x_4 \ \& \ x=x_5)$$
$$\& \ (x)∼((x=x_1 ∨ x=x_2 ∨ x=x_3) \ \& \ (x=x_4 ∨ x=x_5))$$
$$.⊃ ∃!0′′′′′x((x=x_1 ∨ x=x_2 ∨ x=x_3)$$
$$∨ (x=x_4 ∨ x=x_5)).$$

This sentence is false when we assign to $x_1, \ldots, x_5$ five distinct entities of the universe. Once again we see that if the universe is too small then the distribution of truth-values which results from my truth conditions is non-standard; while if the universe is large enough truth-values will be standard, but this will be due to non-mathematical considerations.

It is clear that multiplication, since it is based recursively on addition, must inherit the latter's difficulties. In general, if the universe contains fewer members than what we call the product of a and b, ⌜Pabc⌝ will be true for all c. So (ii) is verified.

Finally, we need to see that the problem affects even those sentences which are usually taken as axioms of first order number theory. Here are two examples:

(12) (m)(n)(m′=n′ ⊃ m=n)
(13) (m)(n)(r)(Sm′nr′ ⊃ Smnr).

To see the infirmity of (12), imagine the universe has exactly two members, and consider its instance:

(14) 0′′′=0′′′′ ⊃ 0′′=0′′′.

The antecedent is (8) which is true in such a universe, but the consequent is false: via (=) its truth condition is '(F)(∃!0′′xF ≡ ∃!0′′′xF)' which fails when 'x = x' is the substituend for 'F'. In general, (12) will hold up to the point where the universe has at least as many things as the minimum of the numerals in its antecedent and then will fail. For (13), suppose the universe has exactly four things and consider the following instance of (13):

(15) $S0'''0''0''''' \supset S0''0''0'''''$.

The antecedent is (10) which is true in such a universe, but the consequent is false: any two open sentences whose extensions are two-membered and disjoint will falsify it. The moral here is the same as before: either the universe is not big enough, in which case these two standard axioms of number theory are false according to my assignment of truth conditions, or it is big enough, but then they are true for non-mathematical reasons. This verifies (iii).

I will argue shortly that (ii) and (iii) are results which are to be welcomed, but before I do so, I want to define the apparent difficulty precisely. It appears that what is needed is an axiom of infinity in order to restore standard truth-values, and thus this problem is identical to the problem which has plagued foundations of mathematics from Frege and Russell onwards. This is only half true. There are two philosophical objections to an axiom of infinity in settings other than the theory offered in this chapter: (a) the axiom requires the existence of an infinity of *things*, and (b) the axiom requires the existence of *numbers*. The axiom generates (a) and (b) by asserting that there is an infinity of numbers, but the objections are separable. I for one would not be satisfied to see a method whereby (a) is avoided if we are still required to assume the existence of (even a finite number of) numbers, if they are conceived to be abstract entities. Likewise, it will not do to somehow avoid commitment to abstracta if the account of arithmetic requires the assumption that there is an infinity of things (other than numbers). The reason is twofold. First, it might be false. And second, even if it is true, it is not the business of arithmetic to assert it. Roughly, the problem is that to make arithmetic so depend would be to distort its epistemic status in such a way as to wreak havoc with our traditional network of justification upon which much of our knowledge depends. This, then, is the problem which my assignment of truth conditions faces. Nor will it do to take a sentence which asserts that there is an infinity of things and add it as an antecedent to each of the axioms of number theory. For then each theorem will require the same prefix, and so in order to assert that two plus four is not seven, or even that one differs from two, we will have to know that the universe is infinite (in order to detach the antecedent).

Now for the defence of (ii) and (iii). I will argue that (ii) is precisely what is to be expected if we found our account of arithmetic upon its application to multiplicity attributions, and thus (ii) is to be welcomed. (iii) requires revision of the axioms for number theory. This will be accomplished in such a way as to avoid an axiom of infinity; rather I will add to (12) and (13) (the rest of the axioms are acceptable as they stand) antecedents which express the needed requirement *for each instance independently* in such a way that the resulting axioms, like the rest of the axioms for number theory, will be logically true.

For the defence of (ii) I will here focus solely on the application of arithmetic to multiplicity attributions; other putative applications will be considered in later chapters. First consider the distribution of truth-values to atomic identities. The function of numerals in this application of arithmetic is to record the multiplicity of open sentences by taking their place in exclamation sentences. Via (R1), the numerals indicate a context-dependent combination of quantifiers and identity which, for any given open sentence of L0, asserts that it has a particular multiplicity. If a and b are such that $\ulcorner \exists !axF \urcorner$ and $\ulcorner \exists !bxF \urcorner$ have the same truth-value no matter what open sentence of L0 replaces 'F', then they are equivalent with respect to the function of recording the multiplicities of predicates. And if that is their only function, then for the purposes of arithmetic there is no need to distinguish between them. Accordingly I allow $\ulcorner a = b \urcorner$ to be true, and have as a result the interchangeability of a and b throughout AL0 *salva veritate*. Numerals which count the same predicates have the same application and hence are equivalent for arithmetic. Thus my response to the possibility of $0''' = 0''''$ coming out true is this: if it comes out true, then it ought to—it can only come out true if there is no open sentence with respect to which $0'''$ and $0''''$ differ, and in that case they are application-equivalent. Therefore, I will take care to avoid axioms for number theory which have $0''' \neq 0''''$ and other sentences like it as unconditional theorems. Since I thus divest myself of responsibility for their truth, I do not have to worry about the fact that they may be false. And even if they are true, this will be for non-mathematical reasons.

In fact, in the case of $0''' = 0''''$ and its ilk I can make an even stronger case. For, as we saw, that sentence will be true iff *neither $0'''$ nor $0''''$ counts any open sentence whatsoever*, i.e., iff *neither $0'''$ nor $0''''$ has any application*. Thus the truth conditions for sentences of the form $\ulcorner a = b \urcorner$ provide the standard truth-values for all numerals which have application; all others are identified under '='. From the applicational point of view, this seems perfectly satisfactory.

It may be objected that there is a difference between the behaviour of a numeral in counting open sentences and its use in *asserting* the multiplicity of open sentences. Thus, even though there are circumstances in which $0'''$ and $0''''$ will count exactly the same open sentences (i.e. when neither counts any open sentence), what $0'''$ and $0''''$ assert concerning the multiplicity of any open sentence is quite different: '∃!$0'''$xF' and '∃!$0''''$xF' are logically incompatible. Why shouldn't this difference which they contribute to the content of multiplicity attributions be recorded by '='? In order to answer this objection, let's distinguish between equivalence with respect to actual and potential applications. Two numerals are equivalent with respect to actual applications iff they count the same open sentences *in the real world*; they are equivalent with respect to potential applications iff they *would* count the same open sentences *no matter how the world was*. Now '=' under my truth conditions registers equivalence with respect to actual applications. This accords with my thoroughly pragmatic view of arithmetic: it must be sufficient to get me through this world; others, possible though they may be, cannot be *needed* to understand what arithmetic says. (This is not to say that the believer in possible worlds cannot use my account of arithmetic in describing those worlds; obviously he can. But I don't want to be *committed* to those worlds in explaining how we use arithmetic in *ours*.) Of course, it is quite true that $0'''$ and $0''''$ have different *meaning*. Since '∃!$0'''$xF' and '∃!$0''''$xF' are logically incompatible and they differ only with respect to $0'''$ and $0''''$, $0'''$ and $0''''$ cannot be synonymous. The difference is easily explicable by appeal to the semantical rule (R1) and the semantics for L0. But it does not follow that $0''' \neq 0''''$ must be unconditionally true unless we expect '=' to register all differences in meaning, and we don't expect that: in the usual accounts of arithmetic '2 + 2' and '3 + 1' differ in meaning even though $2+2 = 3+1$. Thus the mere fact that '=' equates numerals which differ with respect to meaning and potential applications will not be an objection.

The same rationale applies to standardly false sentences of the form ⌜Sabc⌝. How is addition applied to multiplicity attributions? When two open sentences of L0 are disjoint, addition co-ordinates the numerals which count them with the numeral which counts their disjunction. This means that a sentence of the form ⌜Sabc⌝ has application iff there are two disjoint open sentences of L0 which a and b (respectively) count. Now this is precisely the condition under which sentences of that form will have the standard distribution of truth-values, as can be seen by considering their truth condition:

(16)   (F)(G)((∃!axF & ∃!bxG & ~(∃x)(F & G)) ⊃ ∃!cx(F ∨ G)).

If the condition is met, then there is an instance of the antecedent of (16) which is true, and then the consequent of (16) is refuted by its antecedent (making (16) as a whole false) unless c is the numeral which gives the standard sum of a and b (in which case the consequent, and (16) as a whole, are true). If the condition is not met, then there is no true instance of the antecedent of (16) and so (16) is true no matter what its consequent is. This means that iff there is no application for the addition of a and b will ⌜Sabc⌝ be true no matter what c is; while iff there is an application for the addition of a and b will ⌜Sabc⌝ be true just for the standard choice of c.

Thus suppose it is objected: we know that S0″0″0‴, but for all we know about arithmetic S0″0″0‴ might also be true: how then do we know upon which to rely when actually applying arithmetic? If we do not know that the latter is false then we have two different sums for 0″ plus 0″; why do we assume that the first is correct and the second incorrect instead of the opposite? (We could point out that S0″0″0‴ is *logically* true while S0″0″0‴, if true at all, is only contingently true, but this might not satisfy the questioner: he might insist that we need to know for sure that one answer is wrong in order to wholly rely upon the other—knowing that one answer is correct for sure and other only *might* be correct would not suffice.) The answer is that S0″0″0‴ is only true if there is no application whatsoever for the sum of 0″ and 0″ hence there is no applicational situation in which we could worry concerning which answer to apply.

For the same reason we need not worry that shrinkage in the universe—i.e., some of its members ceasing to exist—will result in new truths of addition which will compete with the old: the competition is unreal since the shrinkage creates new truths only if it makes them totally inapplicable. (Of course, we could also reply by letting our variables range over the entire contents of space-time—a sound policy in any case—and then questions of change in the size of the universe from time to time disappear.)

Suppose someone objects: it is of interest to me to do sums not only with respect to what there is in the world, but with respect to what there might be, especially if it is up to me whether they will be or not. For example, I have to provide boxes for a lot of 25 cameras; I have 16 boxes in the storeroom; how many boxes shall I make? This application of addition is not obviously on a par with finding the multiplicity of two open sentences whose multiplicities are already fixed. Nevertheless, it can be analysed in terms of 'S' under my truth conditions. Since the universe contains the 25 cameras, the addition of any two numerals whose standard sum is 25 or less has application. And then there is a unique a such that $\ulcorner$S16a25$\urcorner$ is true. Thus there is a unique a such that $\ulcorner(\exists!ax(x$ is a box I will make) iff I will have exactly one box per camera$)\urcorner$ is true, and that a tells me how many to make. Suppose the objector tries again: the camera case succeeded only because you had the 25 cameras to start with. Suppose I am considering whether or not to make cameras: I know that currently there are m cameras in existence, and I want to know how many there will be if I make n more (I am afraid of exceeding the market, say). Don't we have to worry that the standard sum of m and n will exceed the size of the universe and then there will be no unique c such that $\ulcorner$Smnc$\urcorner$ is true? No, we don't. For there is only one c which allows both $\ulcorner$Smnc$\urcorner$ and its antecedent to be true; the others can only be true iff their antecedents are uniformly false, i.e. iff the sum of m and n has no application. Now in this circumstance, this means that they can be true only if I do not make the n cameras! The only true sentence $\ulcorner$Smnc$\urcorner$ which is consistent with that assumption is the standardly true one, hence it is the only one to take account of in making my plans.

The case of multiplication is handled directly by the rationale for addition. To sum up: the defence of (ii) is simply that whenever numerals, addition, and multiplication have application then the distribution of truth-values under my truth conditions is standard; when they do not, some standardly false sentences are true, but this is of no consequence. This rationale may be put in a general and precise form as follows. Let the *set of target conditionals* for an open sentence ϕmnr of AL0 be the set of all sentences of the form $\ulcorner$Applicable $(\phi$mnr$) \supset \phi*$mnr$\urcorner$ where the antecedent in place of 'Applicable $(\phi$mnr$)$' expresses the conditions of applicability of ϕmnr, and in place of '$\phi*$mnr' is either $\ulcorner\phi$abc$\urcorner$ in case $\ulcorner\phi$abc$\urcorner$ is standardly true, or $\ulcorner\sim\phi$abc$\urcorner$ in case $\ulcorner\phi$abc$\urcorner$ is standardly false. The distribution of truth-values will agree with the standard distribution whenever ϕmnr is applicable just in case all the target conditionals are true. The argument so far has shown that this is the case for '=', 'S', and 'P'.

Actually, we can set a much stronger requirement. We may demand in addition that the target conditionals be expressible in AL0 and that they be *logically* true. The motivation for this demand is that we be able to replace the over-strong, unconditional theorems whose truth depends on my view upon the conditions for application being met with weaker theorems having the conditions of application as antecedent. This demand can be met. Let's start with '='. Its condition of application is simply that the numerals which flank it have application, for only under that condition can their equivalence have an impact on registering multiplicities. We may express the applicability of a numeral a as $\ulcorner a \neq a' \urcorner$. For, its truth condition is $\ulcorner (\exists F) \sim (\exists!axF \equiv \exists!a'xF) \urcorner$ which is equivalent to $\ulcorner (\exists F)(\exists!axF \lor \exists!a'xF) \urcorner$; and both disjuncts guarantee a application. (If $\ulcorner \exists!axF \urcorner$ is true, then a applies directly to F, while if $\ulcorner \exists!a'xF \urcorner$ is true, then a gets relational application in $\ulcorner (\exists y)\exists!ax(x \neq y \ \& \ F) \urcorner$.) Thus the target conditionals for '=' are of the form $\ulcorner (a \neq a' \ \& \ b \neq b') \supset (a = b)^* \urcorner$ where the consequent is $\ulcorner a = b \urcorner$ or $\ulcorner a \neq b \urcorner$ depending upon whether or not $\ulcorner a = b \urcorner$ is standardly true. As we saw just above, the applicability condition for 'S' is simply that the antecedent of (S) have a true instance, viz. $\ulcorner (\exists F)(\exists G)(\exists!axF \ \& \ \exists!bxG \ \& \ \sim(\exists x)(F \ \& \ G)) \urcorner$. This can be expressed in AL0 as $\ulcorner (\exists n) \sim Sabn \urcorner$, since the latter will be true iff its antecedent has a true instance. And thus the target conditionals for 'S' have the form: $\ulcorner (\exists n) \sim Sabn \supset (Sabc)^* \urcorner$. 'P' is handled similarly. The logical truth of the target conditionals is demonstrated in the Appendix.

The expressibility of the target conditionals in AL0 and their logical truth is all that is needed to show that the truth conditions are indeed appropriate to arithmetic as applied to multiplicity attributions. This standard will be employed below to cement the applicational rationale of extensions of the theory of numbers in AL0. Specifically, the method for defining new terms in the theory of natural numbers, and the extension to the theory of rational numbers, will be justified in this way.

(3) Objections

Whatever the merits of my defence of (ii), in the minds of some (ii) automatically brands my version of arithmetic as second best: if we could find truth conditions for the atomic sentences of AL0 which could be used to ground the semantics for AL0, avoided commitment to numbers, and delivered the standard distribution of truth-values, that would surely be preferable. Truth conditions purporting to fill this bill have been suggested by Charles Parsons.[4] All that is needed is an algorithm A for the atomic sentences of AL0 which discriminates the truths from the falsehoods—and we know that there are such—and take

(*)   S is true iff $A(S) = T$

as the assignment of truth conditions for the atomic sentences of AL0 (where '$A(S) = T$' represents a designated outcome of applying the A to S). No reference is made to numbers, and we get the standard truth conditions: isn't (*) ideal? No, for two reasons. (1) Until the algorithm is actually described, we cannot be sure that reference to numbers (or other entities equally objectionable) has really been avoided. Obviously we will not be able to formulate A as a recursive function, and the language of Turing machines either is understood arithmetically or refers to queer things called "machine states" and the like. We might imagine A given as a set of instructions for the manipulation of symbols with '$A(S) = T$' a designated symbolic outcome. But then we cannot say that S is true iff the application of A to S *actually yields* T since A may never actually be applied to S; and the natural temptation to use a subjunctive formulation ("S is true iff A would yield T if it were applied to S") has a high conceptual cost: we now need to understand subjunctive conditionals in order to understand the atomic sentences of AL0. (2) Whether or not it is agreed that the use of arithmetic with respect to multiplicity attributions justifies the non-standard truth-values of my account, *some* account of the application of arithmetic must at least be consistent with the assignment of truth conditions to AL0's sentences. Furthermore, that assignment will have to play a central role in the account of applications. For, as Dummett stresses (cf. chapter IV), to take the assignment of truth conditions as central to semantics is to commit oneself to using the truth conditions of a sentence as *the* feature of the sentence which explains the sentence's role in communication, language learning, and the like. For AL0 this will require accounting for the intimate relations between its atomic sentences and multiplicity attributions, since the uses of numerals in counting, adding, and multiplying are part of one integrated mastery of a part of our language. An assignment of truth conditions to the atomic sentences of AL0 which makes those

[4] Parsons, 1971 [33], 231, n. 1.

relations a mystery will not function as semantics for AL0 in Dummett's sense. This seems to me to disqualify (*), and indeed any truth conditions which do not have a clear route to applications.

Having disposed of the presumed ideal interpretation (*) we must now face the challenge of those who feel the effort is futile. They claim that it is impossible in any case to completely avoid commitment to ordered abstracta in our total theory of the world. The semantical interpretation of substitutional quantification itself, they claim, requires such a commitment when it specifies the substitutional class for the numerical quantifiers. And once we recognize the existence of such entities in whatever context we might as well take them as the natural numbers and use the standard account of arithmetic. If we press the metaphysical and epistemological difficulties of the window view of mathematics, they reply that though those difficulties are undoubtedly genuine, they will apply to the use of abstracta in semantics as well, and since we are forced to use them there we will have to solve (or acquiesce in) those difficulties eventually, and we may expect the resolution of the problems for semantics to apply as well to the use of abstracta in mathematics. Thus there is no need to invent a new interpretation of arithmetic with non-standard truth conditions for the sole purpose of avoiding reference to the abstracta we will have to acknowledge anyway.

There are two ways to respond to this challenge. First, we might try to meet it on its own ground. The use of abstracta in semantics may well be more tractable to explanation than the use of abstract numbers in mathematics. Semantics will require expression types as its abstracta; these may be construed as the shapes (visual, auditory, etc.) of tokens. Thus they are properties instantiated directly by objects, only one step removed from the concrete. Some contend that they will play a role in an account of perception.[5] Numbers, by contrast, are at least two steps from the concrete: numbers register the multiplicity of *classes* of things. They thus require a double abstraction. Nor are they likely to be needed in an account of perception. And the usual set-theoretical reductions of numbers make matters worse; they employ *pure* sets which have no ground whatsoever in the concrete. Thus there is some hope that the problem of abstracta in semantics may receive an independent solution.[6]

[5] Parsons, 1971 [34].
[6] Dummett, 1973, chapter 14, and Jubien, 1977 for a discussion of relative abstractness.

Second, it must be remembered that the nominalization of arithmetic brings tremendous benefits to the philosophy of mathematics—the easing of metaphysical and epistemological concerns noted at the beginning of this chapter. Even if overall nominalism is unworkable, there is no point in freely expanding the pernicious effects of abstracta in an area for which a nominalistic alternative is available. Thus the mere fact that for the sake of semantics we may need to admit the existence of an ordered infinity of abstracta is no reason to use those abstracta to model first order arithmetic if, as is the case, we will lose both our account of arithmetic as a part of logic and our account of its application.

A final objection concerns my use of the notion of logical truth. How can a nominalist define logical truth? Without sets, we cannot appeal to truth in all interpretations. And the definition in terms of truth preserved by substitution has a technical infirmity which is directly relevant to arithmeitc as here construed; for some languages it marks logically true sentences which are not provable in the first order calculus (and hence are not model-theoretically valid). For example, suppose a language L has no (primitive or non-primitive) predicates with infinite extension. Then if F is a predicate of L, the following sentence of L is one whose truth is preserved by substitution, and yet is not regarded as logically true:

$$\sim((x)(\exists y)Fxy \ \& \ (x)(y)(Fxy \supset \sim Fyx)$$
$$\& \ (x)(y)(z)((Fxy \ \& \ Fyz) \supset Fxz)).$$

The usual response is to observe that in any language in which arithmetic can be expressed the substitution definition of logical truth does coincide with first-order provability, and then to remark that all the languages we will be interested in are languages in which arithmetic can be expressed. Apart from the fact that this response does not deal with the theoretical problem of justifying the substitution definition against the charge of misidentifying logical truths, the problem in the context of this chapter is that arithmetic is added in the manner described to a base language *in which arithmetic may not be expressible.* Thus a nominalist cannot simply accept the substitution definition of logical truth for the base language.

It should be understood that whether or not logical truth is a notion available to the nominalist, all the definitions of this chapter will be sound. For, never is logical truth *used* in the definitions. Rather, logical

truth is appealed to in the philosophical analysis of the epistemological status of arithmetic as here construed. Nevertheless, even if the
intelligibility of this construal of arithmetic is not dependent upon a
nominalist analysis of logical truth, its ultimate philosophical interest
may well be. And in any case, surely the nominalist must eventually
address logical theory. In the next few pages I will present an outline
of one possible approach to logical truth. Even in this programmatic
state I hope it will convince the reader that the situation is not
hopeless.

Logic is the theory of argument. Its job is to define such key
characteristics of arguments as validity and soundness, and related
concepts such as consistency, and to provide an explanation of the
uses of valid arguments. The primary locus of logic—the source of its
primitive intuitions and clear cases, and the field of data upon which
its explanatory power must ultimately be tested—is epistemology.
Argument is mainly a method for justifying belief; a successful
argument is one which plays the role in justification which arguments
are meant to play. That role may be roughly characterized as follows.
Arguments are designed to *transfer* justification from premisses to
conclusion, i.e., if one has justified belief in the premisses and believes
the conclusion *on the strength of the argument and the justification of
the premisses* then he *should have* justified belief in the conclusion. If
the argument is successful he *will* have it. *Formal* logic studies those
arguments whose success is due to their form; these arguments are
called (formally) *valid*.

Platonist logic provides the customary definitions of interpretation,
truth in an interpretation, and validity, in terms of set-theoretical
structures. While the resulting theory agrees tolerably well on
cases—it segregates those arguments which are formally successful
from those which are not with reasonable agreement to intuition—the
explanation of the epistemological *use* of valid arguments has never
been worked out in detail. We need to be told how the fact that in no
interpretation are the premisses true and the conclusion false gives the
argument the power to transfer justification in the manner described.
How much help can we expect from the set-theoretical structures
which found the definitions? If we remember our earlier doubts
concerning the value of abstracta in mathematics and semantics, we
may be sceptical. They do provide a mathematically precise
"definition" of "validity" and a rigorous proof of soundness and
completeness for the first order calculus, but all of this constitutes only

the theoretical machinery of logic which must ultimately be applied to the material described in the last paragraph. Otherwise, the entire superstructure becomes irrelevant to *logic*, i.e., to *the theory of argument*.

Sometimes it is suggested that these same structures are the backbone of the theory of truth, which latter is construed as the whole of semantics. Validity, then, is a guarantee given by the very rules of the language that truth will be preserved from the premisses to the conclusion. This idea must be handled with care, lest it revive the cadaver of analyticity, but I think this danger can be avoided (and will hint how shortly). In any case, until we are shown how this appeal to semantics can (must?) make use of the abstracta needed for set-theoretical interpretations, the superstructure still goes begging. In addition, a definition of 'valid argument' in terms of truth preservation guaranteed by semantical rules is in immanent danger of circularity: how shall the "guarantee" be characterized if not by appeal to logical implication? For example, how do the semantical rules for the quantifiers "guarantee" the validity of '$\sim$(x)Fx, therefore ($\exists$x)$\sim$Fx' if not to logically imply that if the premiss is true then the conclusion is true also?

I suggest that we will have a better chance of finding the explanation we seek if we draw our definition from phenomena we wish explained. Instead of casting validity as formal truth preservation and thus involving the theory of truth at the very foundation of logic, we may take validity to be *formal justification preservation*. That is, success is defined as before, and we say that an argument is valid iff every argument sharing its form is also successful. This definition is the very first step in logical theory: it isolates the species of successful argument which logic is to study. 'Horses are mammals, therefore horses are animals', although successful, is not valid—it preserves justification, but not formally; 'Horses are mammals, therefore non-mammals are non-horses' and its ilk are the province of logic. They are so, initially, owing to a rough and ready form we may discern, viz. 'A's are B's, therefore non-B's are non-A's', all of whose instances we judge to preserve justification. (One of the tasks of logic is to provide a *logical grammar*, i.e. an assignment of form to sentences which tallies (for the most part) with our intuitions of formal success. Paraphrase may be needed, alternately conceived as an account of the deep structure of natural language, or as a retreat to an ideal language.)

The *explanation* of the epistemological properties of valid arguments will be found, I believe, in semantics; but both analyticity and circularity must be avoided. The problems of analyticity are bypassed when we distinguish between 'true/justified by virtue of language', which may be styled *linguistic* truth/justification, and 'true/justified by language *alone*' with the implication that such truth/justification is utterly unempirical, which I shall call *analytic*. Now it is the peculiar epistemological status of the analytic within overall empiricism (not to mention specific pointed arguments) which led to its rejection. Nothing prevents us from rehabilitating the power of language to create truth/justification if such power is firmly divorced from the *a priori*. Our motto is: meaning change cannot be divorced from change of theory, but this does not mean that they cannot be *distinguished*, only that the former cannot occur without the latter. The reason is simply that meaning change is a particular species of theory change; it is a change at a particular (deep) level of theory made for certain specifiable kinds of reasons. Thus linguistic truth/justification is empirical in the way that deep-theoretical principles are, and semantics should reveal something of its content. The symptom of this realm is that differences over cases create strong pressure for modified translation; the full diagnosis of those differences may call for sharply divergent semantical interpretations of the language in question. Logic is paradigmatic of the linguistic realm. Disagreement over the validity of arguments which survives intelligent scrutiny will be interpreted as a sure sign of misunderstanding, and the semantics for intuitionistic logic and "quantum logic" show how deep the differences go. The appeal to semantics, then, does not attempt to make logic free from empirical pressures, but rather to delineate the kind of empirical status it has. Circularity is avoided because we are not *defining* validity via a semantical *guarantee* (which guarantee inevitably involves logic) but rather *explaining* the epistemological status of logic by appeal to the eimpirical pressures upon semantics.

Validity may be connected with truth, as follows. First, note that for any sentence A, ⌜A, therefore 'A' is true⌝ and ⌜'A' is true, therefore A⌝ are successful arguments. Thus if an argument ⌜A, therefore B⌝ is valid, the associated argument ⌜'A' is true, therefore 'B' is true⌝ is successful. Now the success of this latter argument counsels us to transfer justification from ⌜'A' is true⌝ to ⌜'B' is true⌝, and since justification is the guide for rational belief, we are being counselled to accept ⌜'B' is true⌝ whenever we accept ⌜'A' is true⌝. It follows that ⌜A ⊃ B⌝ is to be accepted unconditionally: the success of the argument guarantees this sentence's truth. Here, then, is a sentence whose acceptability—i.e., the justification for its acceptance—is of a piece with the successfulness of arguments; i.e., they have the same epistemological status. Such sentences may be called *logical truths*. But it must be remembered that what logic provides for them directly is justification for their acceptance via the success of the associated argument, and thus the account of that success outlined above will double as an account of the justification we have for accepting those sentences. One final detail: what of logical truths whose main connective is not horseshoe? For such sentences, there is a slightly less direct route from argumental validity to truth. Take ⌜A ∨ ∼A⌝ for example. Arguments of the form ⌜A, therefore A ∨ ∼A⌝ and ⌜∼A, therefore A ∨ ∼A⌝ are valid, and their associated conditionals ⌜A ⊃ (A ∨ ∼A)⌝ and ⌜∼A ⊃ (A ∨ ∼A)⌝ are logical truths. ⌜(A ⊃ B, ∼A ⊃ B, therefore B)⌝ is a valid argument form, and thus its particularization ⌜A ⊃ (A ∨ ∼A), ∼A ⊃ (A ∨ ∼A), therefore A ∨ ∼A⌝ is also valid. Now valid arguments permit transfer of justification, and since the premisses are logical truths, the conclusion receives the unique type of justification which characterizes logical truths, and hence *is* a logical truth. This procedure, it appears, will capture the traditional class of logical truths.

Notice that, although logic is still formal on this account, the objection to the substitutional definition of logical truth no longer applies. Re-cast with respect to validity, the problem was that in a language all of whose predicates have finite extension the following argument is formally truth preserving, and hence valid:

(x)(y)(Fxy ⊃ ∼Fyx)
(x)(y)(z)((Fxy & Fyz) ⊃ Fxz)
Therefore, ∼(x)(∃y)Fxy.

When we shift to the new definition we require for validity not merely preservation of truth but preservation of justification. It is clear that the premisses of this argument may be justified without the conclusion of being so.

Finally, what is the status of the calculus? It is lovely to have a reasonably practical method for discovering which arguments are valid, but this should be regarded as an accident when it occurs. First order logic is simply lucky to have a semi-decision procedure; monadic first order logic is luckier still in being decidable, and the logic of branching quantifiers and second order logic are less lucky in being not even semi-decidable. It is no more a requirement of logic that it provide a mechanical procedure for identifying, or generating, the valid arguments, than it is a requirement of a theory of mathematics that it do so for the mathematical truths. Nevertheless, it is comforting to note that the first order calculus can be used freely on the present approach, for it may be proved inductively that it is sound with respect to validity as here defined. The question of completeness will have to wait for further investigation.

This sketch will have to suffice for now. The key idea is that validity and logical truth are characterized directly in epistemological terms and semantics is cited as the epistemological type under which logic falls. It is to be hoped that set-theoretical constructions can be avoided in semantics. If they can, logic will be placed on a sound nominalistic footing.

(4) Axioms for Number Theory in AL0

If the defence of (ii) is accepted, we see that the approach to (iii) must be to revise the standard axioms for first order number theory. For, the possible falsity of the axioms (12) and (13) is a result solely of the possibility of non-standard truth-values for unquantified simple sentences of AL0: the fact that the quantifiers are substitutional means that the truth-value of quantified sentences depends solely on the truth-values of their unquantified instances. And since we have justified (ii) we must acquiesce in the possible falsity of (12) and (13) and then, since we do not want axioms subject to this infirmity, they will have to be replaced. Our guide in finding their replacement must be the same as the rationale which justified (ii): in every case where identity, addition, and multiplication have application the ordinary theorems must follow from the axioms.

Let's start with (12) $((m)(n)(m'=n' \supset m=n))$. The problem with (12) is that it (together with '$(n)(0 \neq n')$' which will be accepted as an axiom) logically implies all sentences of the form $\ulcorner a \neq b \urcorner$ where a and b are different numerals. These are among the sentences which, although standardly true, are possibly false on my theory. However, they are only false if neither a nor b has any application, i.e., if neither counts any predicate. Thus all sentences of the form

$$(17) \quad ((\exists F)\exists!axF \lor (\exists F)\exists!bxF) \supset a \neq b$$

where a and b are different numerals are logically true, since the antecedent expresses the applicability of a or b. Now in general

⌜a≠a'⌝ logically implies ⌜(∃F)∃!axF⌝, thus

(18)   (a≠a' ∨ b≠b') ⊃ a≠b

is also logically true, and it expresses within the vocabulary of AL0 precisely what is desired: when either a or b has application (and a and b are different numerals) ⌜a ≠ b⌝ is true. An axiom which has all sentences of form (18) as logical consequences is desirable, and it is obvious that what we want is

(19)   (m)(n)(((m≠m' ∨ n≠n') & m'=n') ⊃ m=n).

(19) (together with '(n)(0 ≠ n')') enables us to prove all instances of (18), but no instances of ⌜a ≠ b⌝ *simpliciter*. That (19) is logically true will be shown in the Appendix.

Now consider (13)((m)(n)(r)(Sm'nr' ⊃ Smnr)). The problem with (13) is that if (a,b) is the largest pair of numerals whose sum has application, then ⌜Sa'bc⌝ will be true for all c, while there will be exactly one c which makes ⌜Sabc⌝ true. Thus for all but one choice of c the antecedent of (13) will be true and the consequent false when a and b are substituted for 'm' and 'n' respectively. What is needed is the additional assumption that the addition of ⌜a'⌝ and b has application, i.e., the assumption that

(20)   (∃F)(∃G)(∃!a'xF & ∃!bxG & ~(∃x)(F & G))

is true. Now (20) is logically equivalent to

(21)   ~(F)(G)((∃!a'xF & ∃!bxG & ~(∃x)(F & G))
       ⊃ ∃!cx(F ∨G))

as long as c is *not* the standard sum of ⌜a'⌝ and b. (Proof: if c is not the standard sum of ⌜a'⌝ and b then the antecedent of (21) (minus its negation) and its consequent are logically incompatible, hence the antecedent logically implies the negation of the consequent. So when we push the negation through we get the antecedent conjoined with the negation of the consequent; since the former logically implies the latter, the latter may be dropped and the result is (20).) And (21), via (S), is the truth condition of

(22)   ~Sa'bc.

So we see that the addition of ⌜a'⌝ and b has application iff ⌜~Sa'bc⌝ is true for some c. Thus the modification of (13) is:

(23)   (m)(n)(r)(((∃t)~Sm'nt & Sm'nr') ⊃ Smnr).

The point of (13) was to enable us to take a single theorem of the form $\ulcorner{\sim}Sabc\urcorner$ and derive an infinity of consequences: $\ulcorner{\sim}Sa'bc\urcorner$, $\ulcorner{\sim}Sa''bc''\urcorner$, ... (23) allows us to do the same thing as long as we have the additional assumption at each stage that the addition of the first two numerals has application.

The rest of the axioms of number theory are standard. They are:

$(n)(0 \neq n')$
$(n)S0nn$
$(m)(n)(r)(Smnr \supset Sm'nr')$
$(n)P0n0$
$(m)(n)(r)(Pm'nr \equiv (\exists t)(Pmnt\ \&\ Stnr))$
$(n)(n = n)$
Axiom schema of substitution
Axiom schema of induction.

These will be shown logically true in the Appendix. Together with (19) and (23), they suffice to prove all the classical theorems of number theory with the qualification that some require prefixes which express the applicability of the numerals and operations they contain. We must now evaluate this account with respect to the traditional objections to axioms of infinity, and with respect to the objection that weakening of the traditional axioms automatically rules such an account out of court.

I am certainly not using an axiom of infinity, since all my axioms are logically true (and here logic means first order logic—extended to include infinite bundles of first order logical truths). Furthermore, I have not used an assumption of infinity as a prefix for my axioms and theorems. It cannot be claimed that we must know that there is an infinity of things before we can know that $\ulcorner 0' \neq 0''''\urcorner$ or $\ulcorner{\sim}S0''0''0'''\urcorner$ are true, since we will have the following theorems:

(24) $(0' \neq 0'' \vee 0'''' \neq 0''''') \supset 0' \neq 0''''$
(25) $(\exists t){\sim}S0''0''t \supset {\sim}S0''0''0''$.

The antecedent of (24) is satisfied iff the universe is non-empty; the antecedent of (25) is satisfied iff there are four or more things in the universe. Thus we may detach the traditional theorems $\ulcorner 0' \neq 0''''\urcorner$ and $\ulcorner{\sim}S0''0''0'''\urcorner$ even if we do not know that the universe is infinite. The infinity problem is here handled piecemeal: each theorem has just enough power in its prefix to guarantee that there are enough things to justify its particular application of '=' or 'S'.

Nevertheless, there are those who will claim that the need for *any* prefix at all disqualifies this account. It is patently obvious, they say, that the traditional theorems of number theory are true and they are indispensable in practice, and (24), (25), and so on are not adequate substitutes. Obviously I cannot agree with their complaint. But perhaps I can dissipate it by the following observation. In practice we may use the traditional algorithms for addition and multiplication without paying any heed to the extra prefixes which I demand. The reason is that when we do any calculation *which we expect to apply* we are tacitly assuming that the universe contains enough members to make the application possible. That is, we are tacitly assuming that the extra antecedents are true. So we naturally detach them and proceed via traditional number theory. It is obvious that this is perfectly justifiable according to my account. Thus we may see number theory as being used on two levels simultaneously. In everyday life it is used subject to the tacit assumption just mentioned, and hence the traditional axioms are in force and the standard methods of calculation are in order. In theory, when we are asked for theses of AL0 which we can assert unconditionally as starting-points for mathematical proof, we must use the axioms I presented.

(5) *Definitions*

The sensitivity of the unquantified sentences of AL0 to the (non)existence of open sentences of various multiplicities is reflected by a parallel sensitivity of standard arithmetical definitions. Consider, for example, the following:

(26) $a < b = df (\exists n)(Sanb \& n \neq 0)$

(27) $a/b = df (\exists n)(Panb \& n \neq 0)$ (a divides b).

From (26)–(27) it follows that if the universe if finite and non-empty then for all a and b, $\ulcorner a < b \urcorner$ and $\ulcorner a/b \urcorner$ are true. If the universe if finite, then for any a there is a c which will falsify the antecedent of $\ulcorner Sacb \urcorner$, and hence verify the whole; and if the universe if non-empty, then c is not 0; hence $\ulcorner a < b \urcorner$ holds for all a,b by (26). Similarly for (27). These definitions are obviously untenable; what shall we use to replace them?

Adopting the standpoint of section (2), we need definitions which will agree in truth-values with the ordinary definitions of these notions for numerals a,b which are applicable, i.e., which register the multiplicity of some predicate. If they are so applicable, then there is some applicational point to defining the familiar arithmetical notions for them: those notions give us information about the multiplicity relations among our predicates. When we run beyond the applicable numerals, the distribution of truth-values to instances of the defined notions is insignificant. The definitions we want can be formulated by writing into the usual definitions a clause which guarantees applicability at every point in which either 'S' or 'P' is used in the definiens. The clauses in question are as follows: an occurrence of $\ulcorner Sabc \urcorner$ is supplemented with $\ulcorner (\exists n) {\sim} Sabn \urcorner$, and an occurrence of $\ulcorner Pabc \urcorner$ is supplemented with $\ulcorner (\exists n) {\sim} Pabn \urcorner$. Our examples now become:

(26') $\quad a{<}b =df (\exists n)(Sanb \ \& \ (\exists m){\sim}Sanm \ \& \ n{\neq}0)$
(27') $\quad a/b =df (\exists n)(Panb \ \& \ (\exists m){\sim}Panm \ \& \ n{\neq}0)$.

Now if a and b are both applicable, then in order to satisfy (26') there must be some c which verifies the *antecedent* of $\ulcorner Sacd \urcorner$ for some d (otherwise it could not falsify the whole of $\ulcorner Sacd \urcorner$ as the new clause requires); thus there is only one b which will make $\ulcorner Sacb \urcorner$ true—intuitively, the right one, viz. the sum of a and c. (27') is the same. Thus (26') and (27') bring a < b and a/b into line for applicable a,b. Now if either a or b is not applicable, then we still have the result that $\ulcorner a < b \urcorner$ and $\ulcorner a/b \urcorner$ hold for all a,b. But from the applicational point of view this is of no consequence, and so we will tolerate it. Moreover, the same argument indicates that we can apply to (26') and (27') the standard formulated at the end of the section (2): the target conditionals for $\ulcorner a < b \urcorner$ and $\ulcorner a/b \urcorner$ should be expressed in AL0 and logically true. Assuming that '< ' and '/' are applicable whenever the numerals flanking them are (the weakest possible assumption), the target conditionals are

$(a{\neq}a' \ \& \ b{\neq}b') \supset a{<}^*b$
$(a{\neq}a' \ \& \ b{\neq}b') \supset a/^*b$

where the consequents are the definiens of '<' and '/' or their negations, depending upon whether a and b give standardly true or standardly false cases of '<' and '/'. These are shown logically true in the Appendix.

The method employed in these examples is easily applied to the usual run of terms defined in elementary number theory. Nevertheless, the definiens is somewhat unfamiliar and more complicated than usual. The rehabilitation of "inductive definitions" noted in chapter IV affords an alternative method of incorporating all primitive recursive functions. A primitive recursive function may be defined from zero and the successor function via a finite number of applications of projection, substitution, and recursion. First order syntax makes projection and substitution directly available, and inductive definitions simply are recursion. Thus exponentiation may be added to AL0 (which already has addition and multiplication) via the "definition":

$\ulcorner E(a,0,c) \urcorner$ is true iff $\ulcorner c = 0' \urcorner$ is true
$\ulcorner E(a,b',c) \urcorner$ is true iff $\ulcorner (\exists d)(E(a,b,d) \ \& \ Padc) \urcorner$ is true.

This "definition" together with the semantics for the quantifiers gives truth conditions for all sentences in which 'E' appears in terms of sentences which already possess truth conditions. Definitions of this type also pass the target conditional test, as will be shown in the Appendix. It should be noted that if this method is used we will require a continual strengthening of the *axioms* of number theory in AL0. For, each new primitive recursive function is added to AL0 via a new notation which is not given an eliminative definition. What is required is that counterparts of the inductive definitions be added to the axioms to mirror the deductive impact of the usual eliminative definitions. For exponentiation the axioms will be

$(x)E(x,0,0')$
$(x)(y)(z)(E(x,y',z) \equiv (\exists w)(E(x,y,w) \ \& \ P(x,w,z)))$.

Once we have the primitive recursive functions, we may define the general recursive functions by appeal to (25'). For, any general recursive function may be defined by applying a "minimum" operator to a primitive recursive function, and the "minimum" operator for a functional relation Fxy is defined:

z is the least x such that Fxy $=df$ (w)(Fwy $\supset$ z$\leqslant$w) & Fzy.

In sum: although some new techniques are employed, AL0 will be able to provide all the usual defined terms of elementary number theory.

(6) Logicism

I will end this chapter by explaining in what sense my account of number theory can be called "logicism". Certainly my account differs greatly from those of Frege, Russell, etc. They had numbers as entities, axioms of infinity, assumed set theory as part of logic, and had no clear account of the applicability of arithmetic. Furthermore, it should be pointed out that there are at least four different theses which have been traditionally associated with logicism, of which only some are reasonable, and only one is true of my account. They are:

(L1)   All of the standard truths of arithmetic are theorems of some axiomatized pure logic.

(L2)   All of the standard truths of arithmetic are logically true.

(L3)   All of the standard axioms of arithmetic are logically true.

(L4)   All of the sentences of arithmetic which can be justifiably taken as axioms are logically true.

That (L1) is false we know from Gödel's incompleteness theorem. But it is also unreasonable: the heart of logicism is the claim that arithmetic is a branch of logic, i.e., their semantical, epistemological, and metaphysical basis is the same; there is no need to claim that arithmetic is an *axiomatizable* branch of logic for all this to be true. It is enough to have a "translation" of the sentences of arithmetic into the vocabulary of logic which preserves the cognitive role of the former. If we can map the sentences of arithmetic onto sentences which are tautologies of first order logic (or substitutional generalizations of such tautologies) so that logical relations, proof relations (including the epistemic priority of axioms over theorems which enables the former to establish the truth of the latter), and applications are preserved, then we can show that arithmetic may as well be taken as (or: replaced by) those tautologies. The non-existence of an effective proof procedure for this "arithmetical" part of logic is irrelevant to this kind of reduction of arithmetic to logic. On this basis (L2) and (L3) are reasonable, but if "logically true" means "tautologies of first order logic", then we have every reason to think them false. My account verifies (L4). (L4) guarantees that all the sentences of arithmetic which we use in justifying our claims to knowledge—i.e., all sentences of arithmetic which have a cognitive function—are first order tautologies. I think this is sufficient to give us a literal logicism: the use of arithmetic in the pursuit of knowledge is nothing more than the use of (a fragment of) the first order logic of multiplicity attributions. My account does not provide, in itself, an understanding of the epistemological and metaphysical status of arithmetic, but it allows the corresponding foundation for logic to suffice for arithmetic as well; two problems are reduced to one.

VII

Beyond the Natural Numbers

Numberless arithmetic is a first step toward numberless mathematics. Even if arithmetic were the end of the nominalist line, it would be worth the effort: it is important to know precisely where we are compelled to use conceptually and metaphysically high-powered apparatus in our theory of the world. Nevertheless, at whatever point we introduce abstract objects as the subject matter of mathematics we inherit all the difficulties of the window view. It therefore behoves us to see how much we can extend the approach of chapter VI beyond arithmetic. In this chapter a theory of fractions will be defined in AL0 and a few speculations will be appended concerning the future.

The first step is to extend the language AL0 in order to accommodate notation for fractions. This is accomplished by adding the expressions 'm/n' with 'm' and 'n' replaced by formal numerals. The new expressions are called *fractional numerals* and are allowed to occupy the argument places of '=', 'S', and 'P'. New quantifiers and substituends are not necessary since the quantifiers of AL0 already cover all possible pairs (a,b) which fill the blanks of '—/—'. In other words, the work which would be done by a new quantifier '(∃m/n)ϕ(m/n)' is already done by '(∃m)(∃n)ϕ(m/n)'. The resulting language will be called FAL0 (fractional arithmetic of L0). The semantics for FAL0 includes the semantics for AL0 and new truth conditions for the new atomic sentences, viz. sentences composed of '=', 'S', or 'P' flanked by (one or more) fractional numerals. The criterion such truth conditions must meet is the same as the criterion by which the truth conditions for AL0 were judged: the target conditionals must be formulated in FAL0 and be logically true.

As a first pass, let's consider the hopeful thought that since the arithmetic of fractions can be defined in the arithmetic of the natural numbers in well-known ways, all we have to do is ape those definitions. For example, ⌜a/b = c/d⌝ can be defined via the "cross-product" as a·d = b·c. However, in AL0 the latter is represented by ⌜(∃n)(Padn & Pbcn)⌝ and that, we recall, has some limitations. In particular, if the universe is too small (smaller than a·d or b·c) it is too easy to verify. Of course, this will only disqualify the proposed definition if truth-values are non-standard in a universe which is big enough to supply application for the fractions ⌜a/b⌝ and ⌜c/d⌝. Thus in order to test any proposed definition we must first understand enough about the application of fractions to fix the size of the smallest universe in which a given fraction has application.

The strictest possible proposal for the application of fractions is that a fraction applies in any universe which is (at least) as large as its denominator. (The strictness will show in the target conditionals: the antecedent will be very weak and the conditional will be strong, thus making logical truth as hard to achieve as possible.) I think this proposal is correct. If there are (at least) n things in the universe, then there is a predicate whose (relational) multiplicity is registered by n, and for any m < n there is a predicate whose (relational) multiplicity is registered by m. We ought to be able to use m/n to express the ratio of the multiplicities of two such predicates as follows:

$$(\exists r)(\exists s)(\exists!rxF \ \& \ \exists!sxG \ \& \ r\cdot(m/n)=s).$$

Since this use of fractions is basic and requires a universe no bigger than a fraction's denominator, that is the most we can require of a universe in which a fraction will be applicable. (Strictly speaking, this holds only for proper fractions; application of improper fractions requires a universe as large as the largest numerator. Since this strengthens the applicability requirement, it does not affect anything below.) Now we are in a position to test the "cross-product" definition of identity for fractions. ⌜a/b = c/d⌝ must receive standard truth-values in any universe as big as max(b,d). But the multiplications used in the cross-product are reliable only if the universe is as big as max(a·d,b·c). Thus that definition is unacceptable.

A definition of identity for fractions which is more economical in its use of multiplication is the following, in two steps:

$$a/b == c/d \text{ iff } (\exists n)((a\cdot n=c \ \& \ b\cdot n=d) \lor (c\cdot n=a \ \& \ d\cdot n=b))$$
$$a/b = c/d \text{ iff } (\exists r)(\exists s)((r/s == a/b) \ \& \ (r/s == c/d)).$$

This requires no products larger than max(b,d) and thus succeeds where the first definition failed. Translated into AL0 (with appropriate clauses insuring non-trivial application) they become:

(D1)   a/b = = c/d =df ($\exists$n)((Panc

        & ($\exists$m)~Panm & Pbnd & ($\exists$m)~Pbnm)

        $\vee$ (Pcna &($\exists$m)~Pcnm & Pdnb & ($\exists$m)~Pdnm))

a/b = c/d =df ($\exists$r)($\exists$s)((r/s = = a/b) & (r/s = = c/d)).

The target conditionals by which (D1) is tested have $\ulcorner$(b$\neq$b' & d$\neq$d')$\urcorner$ as antecedent and the definiens (or its negation) as consequent; they are shown logically true in the Appendix.

Addition and multiplication of fractions can be defined similarly, always taking care not to require operations which pass the bounds of the minimum universe in which the fractions are applicable. First, note that a fraction is in lowest terms—$L(a/b)$—iff

    $\ulcorner$~($\exists$n)(n divides a & n divides b & n$\neq$0)$\urcorner$

holds. Now the definitions may be given, again in two steps. Intuitively, addition is formulated thus:

a/b + c/d = = e/f iff ($\exists$m)($\exists$n)($\exists$s)($\exists$t)

   (n·b=f & m·d=f & n·a=s & m·c=t & s+t=e)

a/b + c/d = e/f iff ($\exists$r)($\exists$s)($\exists$t)($\exists$u)($\exists$v)($\exists$w)((r/s = a/b)

   & (t/u = c/d) & L(r/s) & L(t/u) & (r/s + t/u = = v/w)

   & (v/w = e/f))

(First $\ulcorner$a/b$\urcorner$ and $\ulcorner$c/d$\urcorner$ are reduced to lowest terms, then added, and then the result is compared with $\ulcorner$e/f$\urcorner$.) The translation into AL0 is:

(D2)   s(a/b,c/d,e/f) =df ($\exists$m)($\exists$n)($\exists$s)($\exists$t)(Pnbf &

                        ($\exists$r)~Pnbr & Pmdf &

                        ($\exists$r)~Pmdr & Pnas &

                        ($\exists$r)~Pnar & Pmct &

                        ($\exists$r)~Pmcr & Sste & ($\exists$r)~Sstr)

  S(a/b,c/d,e/f) =df ($\exists$r)($\exists$s)($\exists$t)($\exists$u)($\exists$v)($\exists$w)((r/s = a/b) &

                        (t/u = c/d) & L(r/s) & L(t/u) &

                        s(r/s, t/u, v/w) & (v/w = e/f)).

For multiplication we have:

a/b · c/d = = e/f iff a·c=e & b·d=f

a/b · c/d = e/f iff ($\exists$r)($\exists$s)($\exists$t)($\exists$u)($\exists$v)($\exists$w)((r/s = a/b) &

   (t/u = c/d) & L(r/s) & L(t/u) & L(r/u) & L(t/s) &

   (r/s · t/u = = v/w) & (v/w = e/f)).

The translation into AL0 is:

(D3) p(a/b, c/d, e/f) =df Pace & (∃r)~Pacr & Pbdf & (∃r)~Pbdr

P(a/b,c/d,e/f) =df (∃r)(∃s)(∃t)(∃u)(∃v)(∃w)((r/s = a/b) &

(t/u = c/d) & L(r/s) & L(t/u) & L(r/u) &

L(t/s) & p(r/s,t/u,v/w) & (v/w = e/f)).

Finally, we can relate fractions to whole numbers as follows:

(D4) a/b == c =df b=0' & a=c

a/b = c =df (∃r)(∃s)((a/b = r/s) & (r/s == c)).

Notice that (D4) enables (D2) and (D3) to be extended to cover addition and multiplication of fractions and wholes; e.g. S(a/b,c,d/e) iff (∃r)(∃s)((r/s = c) & S(a/b,r/s,d/e)).

So much for the formal arithmetic of fractions. What about their application? We have already seen how they can be used to express ratios of multiplicities of predicates. This is one of the two central uses of fractions; the other occurs in measurement which is the subject of the next chapter. A third use concerns such sentences as

(*) Jack built half a house.

(*) poses surprisingly difficult problems. It does not say that (∃x)(x is a house & Jack built half of x) since no one may have finished the house which Jack started. And while (*) is true iff (∃x)(Jack built x & x is half a house), the latter's second conjunct must be understood as 'x is-half-a-house', i.e. 'x is a half-house', and then we may wonder how we will avoid an infinity of predicates: 'x is a third-house', 'x is a fourth-house', etc. Nor let the trouble be laid at nominalism's door. Even if we hypostesize fractions, the difficulty is not obviously solved. For, if we understand (*) as saying that (∃x)(Jack built x & House (x,1/2)), where 'House(x,1/2)' is a binary relation between x and 1/2 which holds iff x is-a-half-house, then we still have to worry about an infinity of predicates: House (x,m/n), VictorianHouse (x,m/n), LargeVictorianHouse (x,m/n), etc. The problem of analysing (*) is further compounded by the fact that that it does not appear to have many logical relations. I suppose it implies the instances of 'Jack built m/n of a house' in which m/n < 1/2 and is implied by those in which m/n ⩾ 1/2, (thus taking 'half' as 'at least half'), but beyond that (*) seems logically unattached. Thus (*) is a problem for everyone, and since I have no solution, I will ignore it. And since these three are the only applications of fractions of which I am aware, I conclude that my account is as viable as any.

A full arithmetic for the rational numbers which accounts for applications and eschews commitment to abstracta is a strong boost for nominalism. And the resources of languages with substitutional quantification for representing mathematics are still unexhausted. Formally, a certain portion of analysis can also be represented. For, by using substitutional quantifiers with respect to the open sentences of FAL0, we can mimic the constructions of set theory in its treatment of sets of numbers. Sets of sets of numbers can be paralleled by adding still another level of predicate quantifiers, and at this level a certain portion of the theory of the real numbers appears. If we continue to add levels, we obtain a hierarchy of systems whose cumulative effect is what has been called "predicative mathematics". While certain portions of classical mathematics are beyond the reach of such a construction, it is unclear whether any *applicable* portions of mathematics are unreachable. Thus the possibility arises that all applicable mathematics may be nominalizable in languages with substitutional quantification. I will close this chapter with a few remarks on what must be done in order for this possibility to be realized.

The substitutional representation of (predicative) set theory proceeds as follows. Set variables are replaced by (substitutional) predicate variables; '$\in$' by predication; and class abstracts may be eliminated in terms of set variables and '$\in$'. Thus

$$\{x: Fx\} \in \{x: Gx\}$$

becomes first

$$(\exists x)(\exists y)(z)((z \in x \equiv Fx) \ \& \ (z \in y \equiv Gy) \ \& \ x \in y)$$

and then, switching to substitutional predicate variables, becomes

$$(\exists H)(\exists I)((z)(Hz \equiv Fz) \ \& \ (Iz \equiv Gz) \ \& \ I(H)).$$

If we factor out the tautologous elements of the latter, we get

$$G(F).$$

And so

$$\{x: x{=}0\} \in \{x: (y)(y \in x \equiv y{=}0)\},$$

which in set theory is equivalent to the tautology

$(y)(y=0 \equiv y=0),$

will have as its substitutional equivalent

$(y)([x = 0](y) \equiv y=0)$

(where the square brackets represent predication) which reduces to the same tautology.

Certain standard notions and theorems can be formulated and proved with little more than a change in notation. Cantor's theorem, for example, appears as follows. $\ulcorner$F is a 1–1 correspondence between G and H$\urcorner$ is defined:

$$0(F;G,H) =df (x)(Gx \supset (\exists y)(z)((Hz \ \& \ Fxz) \equiv z=y)) \ \& \\ (x)(Hx \supset (\exists y)(z)((Gz \ \& \ Fzx) \equiv z=y)).$$

The "power predicate" of F—i.e., the predicate which takes as verifying substituends precisely the predicates which materially imply F—is defined:

$$PF(G) =df (H)((x)(Hx \supset Fx) \equiv G(H)).$$

Cantor's theorem is then stated:

$$(G)(PF(G) \supset \sim(\exists H)0(H;F,G))$$

and proved in the standard way.

Corresponding to the unlimited (and inconsistent) abstraction principle of set theory, namely

$$(\exists y)(x)(x \in y \equiv \dots x \dots),$$

we have

$$(\exists F)(x)(Fx \equiv \dots x \dots),$$

and the latter is a tautology since whatever open sentence we use to fill the dots will also be a substituend for 'F'. There is, of course, no threat of paradox for the latter principle since the predicates which produce contradictions in the former are not in the language in which the latter is formulated. This is a result of having a hierarchy of levels such that no substitutional variable has as a substituend an open sentence containing a substitutional variable of that level. It is also apparent that the staggering existential assumptions of set theory are not being "hidden" in this tautology. For, the fact that 'F' is a substitutional variable means that is has no ontological commitment at all beyond that of its instances. (This is in sharp contrast to the situation in second order logic.)[1]

The theory of "real numbers" may be initiated as follows. In the usual constructions, a real number is a set of rationals. We mimic it with a predicate of rationals, as follows:

$$R(F) =df (x)(Fx \supset (\exists m)(\exists n)(x = m/n)) \ \& \ (\exists x)Fx \ \& \ (\exists x)\sim Fx \ \&$$
$$(x)(Fx \supset (\exists y)(Fy \ \& \ y > x)) \ \& \ (x)(y)((Fx \ \& \sim Fy) \supset x < y).$$

This is the Dedekind "lower cut" construction. Order for R is defined:

Let $R(F)$ and $R(G)$. Then $F < G =df (\exists x)(\sim Fx \ \& \ Gx)$.

Now we can formulate a principle crucial to analysis: the least upper bound principle. Supposing that $(F)(\phi F \supset R(F))$, we define upper bound:

$$UB(F,\phi) =df (G)(\phi G \supset G \leqslant F).$$

Least upper bound is defined:

$$LUB(F,\phi) =df (G)(UB(G,\phi) \equiv F \leqslant G)$$

The least upper bound principle says:

$$(\phi)((\exists F)UB(F,\phi) \supset (\exists F)LUB(F,\phi)).$$

It is usually proved by defining the least upper bound of ϕ as its "sum set" – in our case, we would use the disjunction of all of ϕ's verifying substituends. This may be defined as

$$[lub\phi](x) =df (\exists F)(\phi F \ \& \ Fx).$$

The difficulty is that, as so defined, lubϕ is not a substituend of 'F' in the least upper bound principle since it contains the variable 'F' itself. Thus it cannot be used to prove that principle. Nevertheless, even without the use of the least upper bound principle impressive parts of classical analysis can be developed. Furthermore, additional levels can be added to add strength to the system, forming an unending (and perhaps transfinite) hierarchy. Whether any mathematics needed for science escapes this system is today an open question.

Lest we nominalists rejoice prematurely, I must stress that the above is only a sketch of the *formal* development of "predicative mathematics". What is needed in addition is a study of the *applic-*

---

[1] Quine, 1973 [43], 66–8; Boolos, 1975.

ability of these constructions, especially in the light of the sensitivity of its base—i.e., the sentences of FAL0—to the size of the universe. When real arithmetic and the theory of real functions are developed, each step will have to be checked for adequacy with respect to applications: the target conditionals must be formulated and proved. (Hopefully they can be shown tautologous, thereby rendering *all* of applicable mathematics a branch of logic.) It is likely that some weakening of the traditional axioms will be in order, just as it was for arithmetic, and this weakening will have to be justified in terms of applications. The task is clearly a large one, but so clearly is the anticipated payoff. From this chapter and the last we have at least a clear picture of our resources and the criteria we must meet if a nominalist mathematics is to become a reality.

Aiming, as I am, at a nominalist reconstruction of predicative mathematics, it behoves me to explain why I do not accept Charles Chihara's claim that his system already accomplishes that goal.[2] I have three reasons: (i) his interpretation of quantification appeals to subjunctive conditionals in a way which errs in detail, and in any case such appeal should be rejected in principle; (ii) he appeals to the concept of truth in stating the truth conditions for the sentences of mathematics, thus putting in question the status of his "semantics" for the language of mathematics; (iii) his account of the subject matter of mathematics seems to make an account of applicability untenable. Each will be elaborated briefly.

Chihara's framework for mathematics is Wang's set theory Σ_ω.[3] Quantifiers are interpreted substitutionally with respect to class abstracts. Thus a sentence of the form '$(\exists a)\phi$' means roughly 'There is a class abstract such that . . . ' . Chihara worries about the commitment to type expressions engendered by 'there is a class abstract . . . ' and seeks to avoid it by appeal to the constructibility of expressions according to the syntactical rules of the language. The revised interpretation of '$(\exists a)\phi$' is expressed by Chihara as follows:

. . . if one were to follow [the syntactical rules] without end, one would eventually construct a true [instance]. One could also interpret the sentence to read: it is possible to construct a true [instance] by following this rule of construction.[4]

[2] See Chihara, 1973, chapter V.
[3] See Wang, 1962, pp. 624–51.
[4] Chihara, 1973, p. 203.

As Timothy McCarthy has pointed out, these two characterizations are not equivalent, and neither assigns truth values in an acceptable manner. The latter, understood literally to mean 'It is possible that there is a true instance' counts true

$$(\exists \alpha)(\alpha \text{ is a non-empty set of unicorns}),$$

since there are possible worlds containing unicorns and true token sentences of the form '——— is a non-empty set of unicorns'. The former characterization, understood literally to mean 'Any complete construction of instances would contain at least one true instance', counts true

$$(\exists \alpha)(\alpha \text{ is a non-empty class of expressions of length} \geqslant n),$$

with any numeral in place of 'n', since a complete construction of instances would produce expressions longer than any fixed length. But both of the displayed sentences are false. Appeal to possible world semantics reveals intuitively what has gone wrong: Chihara's appeal to possible complete constructions is meant to be indexed to the real world, in the following sense: the constructed expressions are taken to describe the real world and yet not to form part of the ontology of the real world. Whether Chihara can express this without explicit appeal to possible worlds, and what the resulting effect upon his system would be, is at present unknown.

Chihara's appeal to the subjunctive is made in an attempt to avoid commitment to expression types. The attempt is to be lauded. But even if the details were repaired, the price of using subjunctives is, in my estimation, too high. Until we have a semantical interpretation for subjunctives, we cannot be sure how they are to be understood, and indeed even whether they are free from hidden commitments to abstracta. The philosophical appeal of nominalism sacrificed if we blithely accept subjunctives as intuitively acceptable primitives. Note also that the insistence by some that subjunctives are necessary for the understanding of science—e.g., for dispositions or laws—is no comfort to Chihara, since his subjunctives concern the *consequences of following rules*. The latter is on a par with logical consequences, perhaps, and has nothing in common with solubility and gravity.

In order to explain (ii) and (iii), we need to see Chihara's semantics for the atomic sentences of Σ_ω. Ignoring the complex indexing of expressions, a sentence of the form '$\{x: Fx\} \in \{x: Gx\}$' is understood as follows. The class abstracts are taken to denote *expressions*, roughly their contained open sentences. '∈' expresses satisfaction. (Thus the open sentence in place of 'Gx' will be "meta-linguistic" in the sense that it will be satisfied by expressions.) And satisfaction is defined in terms of truth: roughly, 'Fx' satisfies 'Gx' iff 'G(Fx)' is true. Now if we stop here, we have the peculiar result that at the end of the chain of equivalents giving the semantical interpretation of an atomic sentence of Σ_ω, we have a sentence still containing the term 'true'. Does this mean that a truth *definition* is impossible? Chihara cannot take the final step from "'G(Fx)' is true' to 'G(Fx)' since the latter is a sentence in the very language for which he is trying to specify a semantical interpretation. (This contrasts sharply with my procedure above; since I have a fully interpreted base language I can add set theory by taking '∈' to be *predication*, and not the *truth of* predication.) Perhaps Chihara is relying on the fact that his inductive truth specification for Σ_ω provides a decision procedure for its atomic sentences; surely that adequately redeems the use of 'true'? But we saw reason to doubt such a claim in the last chapter, since the requirement that the semantical interpretation of a language integrated into a theory of understanding and communication makes the mere *identification* of the truths—even if effective—not obviously suited to this larger task.

Finally, the subject matter of Σ_ω is, on Chihara's interpretation, expressions (some of which are only possible). Even if we admit that metaphysical and epistemological problems with abstracta are bypassed, we may still ask for an account of the applicability of what amounts to an ingrown hierarchy of metalanguages to the rest of the world. Assigning truth-values to strings of symbols which are notationally identical to much of classical mathematics is not enough, if those strings are now understood in a much different sense. It is not obvious how the information gleaned from Chihara's Σ_ω concerning (possible) expressions should be used to find the total of the dimes in my right pocket and those in my left, for example. In his short section on the application of Σ_ω Chihara seems to beg the question by *assuming* that a mathematical formulation of a physical situation can be found in Σ_ω and then arguing merely that the standard classical reasoning can be carried out with respect to that formulation. But the question at issue is precisely this: given Chihara's interpretation of Σ_ω how do we know what sentence of Σ_ω gives the mathematical formulation of the physical situation?

It should be clear that these comments on Chihara's system are not meant as a conclusive argument against its success; all nominalists would rejoice if these problems could be solved. In the meantime, however, the approach of this chapter and the last to reconstructing the language of mathematics is offered as an alternative.

VIII

Numberless Measurement

In the previous two chapters we have an account of the language of the arithmetic of rational numbers which is ontologically neutral and which builds upon certain applications of those numbers in giving truth conditions to the sentences of that language. The applications cited were all of one type: determining the multiplicity of open sentences. In order to sustain the account it should be shown either that these exhaust all the applications of rational numbers (either directly, or by reducing other applications to these), or that other applications exist, but they also can be analysed without recourse to reference to numbers. The latter course requires isolating the new sentence-forms in which numerals and numerical quantifiers appear and providing them with truth conditions uncommitted to numbers. To argue that this has been done exhaustively is very difficult. No matter how many sorts of sentences in which numerals appear we analyse, it always seems possible that there are others which cannot be paraphrased via those already treated. Thus the best I can hope to do is to account for the most outstanding of such sentences and treat new types as they come along.

Sentences expressing measurements present just such a challenge. Consider the following:

(1) John is 6 feet tall
(2) John weighs 126 pounds
(3) X has hardness 3.5 on the Mohs scale
(4) The temperature of this liquid is 35 degrees Centigrade.

It is very difficult to see the numerals in these sentences as measuring multiplicities. This is clearest in (3): that sentence obviously does not assert that any open sentence's multiplicity is measured by '3.5'. It is also clear for (4): we do not believe that there are degrees in nature, so what can '35' be counting? The case of (1) and (2) is less clear. It might be thought that they could be analysed in terms of multiplicity attributions as follows: (1) says that John is divisible into 6 disjoint pieces related linearly each of which is exactly one foot long; (2) says that John is divisible into 136 distinct pieces each of which weighs exactly a pound. But this thought is mistaken, for two reasons. First, according to current physics there is no reason to expect that such an account will give correct truth-values. John is a collection of particles. There may be no way of dividing that collection into 136 pieces exactly equal in weight or six linearly related pieces exactly equal in length. Second, even if our physics were different so that we could assert the requisite divisibility of John with confidence, that confidence would be derived from physics. But this impugns the account as an assignment of truth conditions: presumably our semantics should be independent of any particular physical theory, and so we cannot rely upon physics to certify our choice of truth conditions. Thus (1) and (2) cannot be analysed in terms of multiplicity attribution any more than (3) and (4) can.

Although theories of measurement are usually formulated in terms of abstracta, some stress a feature of measurement which holds out some hope to the nominalist: the existence of a measurable quantity is supposed to be due wholly to the existence of "empirical" relations holding among the objects measured. Thus the hope arises that if a theory of measurement is successful we may use it to find the sentences concerning only physical objects and their relations which give the truth conditions for measurement sentences. Now I cannot adjudicate the various claims to correct theories of measurement. Rather, I will take the theory of Brian Ellis[1] and show that if it is correct then there is no need for ontological commitment to abstracta in order to understand measurement. It follows that as long as that theory is in contention we have reason to believe that this application of numerals can be accounted for in an ontologically neutral manner.

In order to show how Ellis's theory can be used to give numberless truth conditions for measurement sentences, I will first present his theory, offer some minor corrections, and then translate it into a language whose syntax and semantics are first order and whose variables take only physical objects as values. The needed truth conditions will then be apparent.

Let 'q' be a schematic letter replaceable by "quantity words", i.e. words such as 'mass', 'length', 'electrical resistance', etc. Ellis defines

---

[1] Ellis, 1968, chapters I–V.

'quantity' as follows. If the three relations 'greater in q than (+q)', 'equal in q to (=q)' and 'less in q than (−q)' are mutually exclusive, then the trio is called a set of quantitative relationships. A quantity "exists" iff a set of quantitative relationships exists, and an object possesses a quantity iff it enters into such relationships. Ellis emphasizes that it is the relations in extension which define the quantity, not the expressions which have those extensions. Thus if different trios of expressions of the form '+q', '=q', and '−q' have the same extensions they define the same quantity. This is especially important when we have many different "operational tests" for what we intuitively take to be a single quantity. Each of those tests can be used to formulate a different trio of expressions '+q', '=q', '−q', and yet we do not want to say that the quantities are different.

Now for my purposes a definition of quantity which refers to extensions and trios of relations will not do. But we may translate as follows:

(D1)   A dyadic open sentence R *expresses a quantity* q iff R is irreflexive, asymmetric, and transitive, and possesses a paraphrase of the form 'is less in q than'.

The trio of ordering relations can be filled out by defining 'x +q y' as the converse of R; defining 'x has q' as $\ulcorner (\exists y)(Rxy \lor Ryx) \urcorner$; and 'x =q y' as $\ulcorner$x and y have q & ~Rxy & ~Ryx$\urcorner$. Finally, we may say that R and S express the same quantity iff $(x)(y)(Rxy \equiv Sxy)$. Ellis's account of quantity is thus nominalized.

Measurement, according to Ellis, is the assignment of numerals to things according to a rule which is determinative (i.e. the same numerals would always be assigned to things under the same conditions) and non-degenerate (i.e. it allows for the possibility of assigning different numerals to different things or to the same thing under different conditions). Such a rule defines a scale of measurement. However, the rule and the scale are not identical, since if two rules would always lead to the same numerals being assigned to the same things under the same conditions, they are two rules for measuring on the same scale. Now a scale S is said to measure a quantity q iff (i) there is a procedure for measuring on S which applies to every object which occurs in the order of q; (ii) every object measurable on S occurs in the order of q; and (iii) if the objects measurable on S are arranged in the order of the numerical assignments (i.e. according to the standard numerical relation '<') they are also arranged in the order of q. To avoid speaking of rules, scales and procedures, we translate as follows.

(D2) Let R express a quantity q. Then Fxn (an open sentence with one free objectual variable and one free substitutional numerical variable) is a numerical measure for R iff the following holds: $\ulcorner(x)(x$ has $q \equiv (\exists n)Fxn)\urcorner$ (for (i) and (ii) above); $\ulcorner(x)(y)(m)(n)((Fxm \ \& \ Fyn) \supset (Rxy \equiv m{<}n))\urcorner$ (for (iii) above); and $\ulcorner(x)(m)(n)((Fxm \ \& \ Fxn) \supset m{=}n)\urcorner$ (to make Fxn functional).

If desirable, we may say that two numerical measures Fxn, Gxn, for R "express the same scale for R" if under "all" conditions $\ulcorner(x)(n)(Fxn \equiv Gxn)\urcorner$ would hold.

Now we are in a position to apply Ellis's theory (as translated) to the problem of finding truth conditions for measurement sentences. Our ability to measure a quantity depends upon the conditions defined in (D1) and (D2) being met. This means that a measurement sentence of the form 'the measure of the quantity q of x = m' must be understood relative to a choice of R expressing q and a numerical measure Fxn for R. Here are the truth conditions for such sentences:

(TC) $\ulcorner$The measure of the quantity q of an object o (relative to R and Fxn) = m$\urcorner$ is true iff R expresses q & Fxn is a numerical measure for R & $\ulcorner$Fom$\urcorner$ holds.

Let's illustrate this procedure with the measurement of length. 'is less long than' expresses length. 'O is 3 feet long' may be thought of as a quick way of saying that the foot measure of the length of O = 3. If we have a numerical measure Fxn for length in feet, then the truth condition for 'O is 3 feet long' will be ' 'is less long than' expresses length & Fxn is a numerical measure for 'is less long than' & FO3 holds'.

Now since (according to Ellis) all measurement depends upon scales, (TC) will be adequate only if we can nominalize our understanding of the establishment of scales which provide the numerical measures for quantities. The basis for all scales are the scales of fundamental measurement, which Ellis describes as follows. We start with the relations 'is less in q than' ($-q$), 'is equal in q to' ($=q$), and 'is greater in q than' ($+q$), which we are able to determine without performing any measurement. There must be an operation ϕ which combines any two systems s and t having q, into a composite system $\phi(s,t)$ having q, such that the following conditions are satisfied:

(i) If s =q t and u =q v then $\phi(s,u)$ =q $\phi(t,u)$ =q $\phi(t,v)$

(ii) $\phi(s,t)$ +q s

(iii) $\phi(\phi(s,t),u)$ =q $\phi(s,\phi(t,u))$

(iv) If $s_1, s_2, \ldots$ is any set of systems equal in q and t is any other finite system possessing q such that s_1 —q t, then there is a number n such that if the systems $s_1, s_2, \ldots, s_n$ are combined successively by the operation ϕ, the composite system is greater in q than t.

If we think of q as weight and ϕ as combined weighing, or q as electrical resistance and ϕ as wiring in series, then conditions (i)–(iii) are clearly desirable. But (iv) is less clear. Literally taken, it is false, since if s —q t, then $\{s_1 = s\}$ is a set which falsifies it. It seems that Ellis is assuming that the set $\{s_1, s_2, \ldots\}$ is infinite. If so, it is clearly a correct condition, but we cannot tell that its truth is not due merely to falsity of antecedent. The point of (iv) is to help ensure that any object possessing q can be located along a scale of q. To be useful to this end there must be an infinite set $\{s_1, s_2, \ldots\}$ to which (iv) can apply. As we shall see, Ellis assumes this below. If the assumption is not met, Ellis will say that we have only a partial scale. (He admits that most of our scales are only partial.) Thus the account as he presents it, and as we shall follow it, is rather idealized.

Assuming the above conditions are met, a scale of measurement for q is set up as follows. First a system of standards for q is constructed. A system s_1 is chosen as initial standard. Another system s'_1 is found such that s_1 =q s'_1, and then $\phi(s_1,s'_1)$ is formed. We then take any system s_2 such that s_2 =q $\phi(s_1,s'_1)$ (and s_2 may itself be taken as $\phi(s_1,s'_1)$) as the second member of the set of standards. The third member is a system s_3 such that s_3 =q $\phi(s_1,s_2)$, and so on. Similarly, we need to find a pair of systems $s_{1/2}, s'_{1/2}$ such that $s_{1/2}$ =q $s'_{1/2}$ and s_1 =q $\phi(s_{1/2},s'_{1/2})$; a trio of systems $s_{1/3}, s'_{1/3}, s''_{1/3}$ such that they are equal in q and their ϕ-combination is equal in q to s_1; and so on.

Ellis's intention is that there should be (a) an infinite sequence of systems $s_1, s_2, \ldots$ which increase in q by equal intervals, and (b) an infinite sequence of *groups* of systems $\{s_{1/2}, s'_{1/2}\}, \{s_{1/3}, s'_{1/3}, s''_{1/3}\}, \ldots$ which divide the initial standard into ever smaller fractions of the quantity q. However, his formulation of the requirement suffices only for (b). To see the failure of (a), let's take his suggestion and use s_1, $\phi(s_1,s_1') = s_2$, $\phi(s_1,s_2) = s_3$, and so on. This inbreeding of standards—i.e., where s_1 is part of s_2, s_1 and s_2 are parts of s_3, and so on—causes trouble for certain quantities and operations ϕ. If q is weight and ϕ is combined weighing (one of Ellis's own illustrations), then $s_2 = s_3 = s_4 = \ldots$! For, since s_1 is already part of s_2, when we "add" s_1 to s_2 for a "combined" weighing, we have exactly what we had before. What is needed is a stipulation to the effect that when we form each new member of the series (a) we use material entirely distinct from s_1. We may describe the series (a) as follows. We start with the initial standard s_1, a second entirely separate system s_1' such that s_1 =q s_1', and a third system s_2 which is entirely separate from s_1 and such that s_2 =q $\phi(s_1,s_1')$. Then for every n, given the standard s_{n-1} which is entirely distinct from s_1, there must be another system s_n which is also entirely distinct from s_1 and is such that s_n =q $\phi(s_{n-1},s_1)$. Notice that we now have an infinite series of systems uniformly increasing in order of q. Now Ellis claims that this series together with condition (iv) guarantees that for any system t possessing q we can find standards s_i and s_j such that s_i —q t —q s_j. Intuitively this ought to be the case, but the series (a) together with (iv) does *not* ensure this result. The reason is that the antecedent of (iv) requires an infinite sequence of systems which are *equal* in q while the members of (a) *increase* in q. In sum, Ellis's conditions do not accomplish what he obviously wants, and it is not immediately clear how they should be revised.

From Ellis's discussion it is clear that the details of his conditions have no rationale other than to arrive at the following result:

(1) For every (finite) system t possessing q there are standards s_i and s_j such that s_i —q t —q s_j

(2) For any two standards s_i and s_j there is a standard s_k such that s_i —q s_k —q s_j.

The importance of (1) and (2) lies in the fact that together they ensure that the system of standards can measure the amount of q possessed by any system t as closely as we desire (within the limits set by our ability to assess the relation —q). We do this as follows. Given s_i —q t —q s_j, let s_k be as (2) requires, and then use it in place of s_i (s_j) if s_k —q t (t —q s_k) (if neither is the case, i.e. not s_k —q t and not t —q s_k, then we have s_k =q t, so s_k measures the amount of q possessed by t exactly), and repeat the process. Since this is the function of the standards, and (1) and (2) guarantee that this function will be fulfilled,

all we need is a set of conditions implying (1) and (2). Here is one way
to do it. First we assume that there is an operation ϕ satisfying Ellis's
first three conditions, viz.

(i)   If s $=_q$ t and u $=_q$ v then $\phi(s,u) =_q \phi(t,u) =_q \phi(t,v)$
(ii) $\phi(s,t) +_q s$
(iii) $\phi(\phi(s,t),u) =_q \phi(s,\phi(t,u))$.

Then we require that series (a) of standards—with the distinctness
requirement—and series (b) of standards exist. (2) is provable directly
from the existence of series (b). Finally, (1) is obtained by taking it
directly as an ("Archimedean") axiom, i.e., as a requirement on the
"comprehensiveness" of the set of standards. This is what I shall take
as (my reformulation of) Ellis's description of the conditions for fundamental measurement. The problem is to translate these conditions into
a generally nominalist, and in particular numberless, language.

Given a sentence Fxy open only in 'x' and 'y', we introduce the
notion 'there are at least n objects bearing Fxy to each other'
(symbolized '$\exists n(Fxy)$') as follows:

$\ulcorner \exists 0''(Fxy) \urcorner$ is true iff $\ulcorner (\exists x)(\exists y)(x \neq y \ \& \ Fxy \ \& \ Fyx) \urcorner$ is true
$\ulcorner \exists n'(Fxy) \urcorner$ is true iff $(\exists z)(\exists n(x \neq z \ \& \ y \neq z \ \& \ Fxz \ \& \ Fyz \ \& Fzx \ \&$
$\quad$ Fzy $\&$ Fxy$)) \urcorner$ is true.

(The rehabilitation of "inductive definitions" noted in chapter IV
allows us to view '$\exists$—(Fxy)' as fully defined, even when the blank is
filled with a (substitutional) numerical variable, as in '(n)$\exists$n(Fxy)'.)
For an n-ary relation $F(x_1, \ldots ,x_n)$ we define 'there are at least n
objects standing in the relation $F(x_1, \ldots ,x_n)$ to one another' thus:

$\ulcorner \exists 0'[Fx_1] \urcorner$ is true iff $\ulcorner (\exists x)Fx \urcorner$ is true
$\ulcorner \exists n'[F(x_1, \ldots ,x_n,x_{n'})] \urcorner$ is true iff $\exists n[(\exists y)(F(x_1, \ldots ,x_n,y) \ \& \ y \neq x_1$
$\quad \& \ldots \& \ y \neq x_n)] \urcorner$ is true.

It is clear that these notions can be combined, that is for two open
sentences Fxy and $G(x_1, \ldots ,x_n)$, $\ulcorner \exists nx\{(Fxy) \ \& \ [G(x_1, \ldots ,x_n)]\} \urcorner$ is
defined. Finally, we can generalize Ellis's notion of forming compound
quantitative systems as follows:

$$O''(x_1,x_2) = O(x_1,x_2)$$
$$O^{n'}(x_1, \ldots ,x_n,x_{n'}) = O(O^n(x_1, \ldots ,x_n),x_{n'}).$$

These notions are used in (D5) below. We may now turn to the
nominalist rendering of Ellis's account of fundamentally measurable
quantities.

Ellis's conditions (i)–(iii) may be handled directly:

(D3) ϕ is an addition operation with respect to q iff
$(x)(y)(z)(w)(((x =_q y)$ & $(z =_q w)) \supset \phi(x,z) =_q \phi(y,z) =_q$
$\phi(y,w)); (x)(y)(\phi(x,y) +_q x);$ and $(x)(y)(z)(\phi(\phi(x,y),z) =_q$
$\phi(x,\phi(y,z)))$.

Now we need a mechanism capable of generating the (a) series. This is accomplished via the following "inductive definition" schema:

(D4) $\ulcorner S_2 xz \urcorner$ is true iff $\ulcorner (\exists y)((x =_q y)$ & $(z =_q \phi(x,y))$ & dist(z,x) & dist(x,y)) $\urcorner$ is true
$\ulcorner S_n xz \urcorner$ is true iff $\ulcorner (\exists y)(S_n^R xy$ & $(z =_q \phi(x,y))$ & dist(z,x)) $\urcorner$ is true.

$\ulcorner S_n xz \urcorner$ is designed to express the fact that z is equal in q to n times the amount of q in x, even though there may not be n different things equal in q to x. Note the presence of the distinctness requirement. Now we may define:

(D5)   x is an initial set of standards for q iff $(n)(\exists z)S_n xz$ and $(n)[\exists n\{(x =_q y)$ & (dist(x,y)) & $[\phi^n(x_1, \ldots ,x_n) =_q x]\}]$.

The first clause asserts that x is the beginning of an infinite chain of standards increasing constantly by the amount of q possessed by x. The second asserts that for each n there are n distinct systems equal in q whose combination under ϕ is equal to q to x. Thus both the (a) series and the (b) series are available when (D5) is fulfilled. We now incorporate the content of (1) thus:

(D6)   x is an initial standard for an Archimedean set of standards for q iff x is an initial standard for a set of standards for q and $(u)(\exists i)(\exists j)(\exists y)(\exists z)(S_i xy$ & $S_j xz$ & y $-_q$ u $-_q$ z).

According to (D6), in order to generate an Archimedean set of standards for q, the set of standards x generates must provide (at least) one greater and one lesser (in q) for every system possessing q. Finally, we can pull all the definitions together as follows:

(D7)   q is a fundamentally measurable quantity (with respect to ϕ) iff $(\exists x)(x$ is an initial standard for an Archimedean set of standards for q).

The last step in Ellis's explication of fundamental measurement is the provision of a scale of measurement for fundamentally measurable quantities. Intuitively, there are two natural courses to follow. First, we may simply refer to (D2) which gives the general conditions for the adequacy of all scales of measurement. The fact that we are dealing here with fundamental measurement which possesses very rich structure will play no role at all in determining the correctness of a scale: preservation of the order of the quantity by the natural order of the numbers will be sufficient. Second, we may assign members to the standards which reflect how many "units" of q they have where we take the initial standard as having one unit. Thus if x is the initial standard, any z such that $S_n xz$ would be assigned 'n' and similarly for the (b) series. Although some favour the more restrictive method, Ellis argues convincingly that there is no compelling reason to do so. Rather, the choice of scale depends upon overall convenience of computation and formulation of laws, and this cannot be determined in general for all quantities. Thus (D2) remains the definition of the adequacy of a scale of measurement even for fundamentally measurable quantities. Likewise the assignment (TC) of truth conditions for sentences asserting that the measure of a particular quantity (in given units) possessed by an object in n is the same as before.

The series of definitions (D1)–(D7) together with (TC) show that, at least according to Ellis's account of measurement, we do not need to refer to numbers (or numerals) in order to understand the nature of measurement or the content of measurement sentences. It seems to me that the method of translation employed above will work equally well for any account of measurement which has the following feature in common with Ellis's account: measurement is seen as the result of a network of relations among the objects to be measured. Intuitively we think of measurement as the assignment of numbers (or numerals) to objects in a way which reflects that structure, but (D1)–(D7) enable us to formulate the content of such "modelling of structure" without reference to numbers (or numerals).

Patrick Suppes's account of measurement differs from that of Ellis in certain respects, but can be expressed within the framework presented above.[2] Suppes agrees that the point of measurement is to represent empirical relations among physical objects via isomorphic numerical systems, hence (D2) will define the correctness of a proposed scale of measurement for a quantity for him as well as for Ellis. However, Suppes argues that what we have called measurement sentences do not reflect the empirically fundamental stage in the

[2] Suppes, 1959; Suppes and Zinnes, 1963.

description of quantitative relations. The quantitative relations which are wholly empirical are those which are independent of the arbitrary choice of units, origin, etc. which are needed to determine a particular numerical measure. Measurement sentences are dependent for their truth conditions upon such choices, and hence reflect partially empirical, partially conventional states of affairs. Suppes argues that the theory of measurement should start with an account of those sentences which reflect the purely empirical reality (or: quantitative relations independent of conventions determining a particular numerical measure), and then proceed to explain how the conventions we use determine numerical measures for representing that reality.

The distinction between our measurement sentences and the sentences which Suppes regards as fundamental may be illustrated as follows. Consider:

(i)   The mass of a $= 4$
(ii)   The mass of a is greater than the mass of b
(iii) The mass of a $= 5 \cdot$ (the mass of b)
(iv)   The mass of a $= 4$ grams.

Sentence (i) is problematic: as it stands, its content is indeterminate in the sense that no particular facts about a (or anything else) determine its truth-value. It does not have determinate truth conditions; we might say that it is meaningless. What it lacks is a specification of unit. If we understood it as (iv) (say the context made clear what units were pre-supposed), then there would be no problem since (iv) has perfectly determinate truth conditions. On the other hand, numerically exact facts about a quantity such as mass do not have to wait on a choice of unit: (ii) and (iii) also have determinate truth conditions despite the fact that no unit is specified. Suppes's approach is to declare (i) meaningless, relegate (iv) to a later stage in the account of measurement; and to start by explaining the use of (ii) and (iii) in describing purely empirical quantitative relations. To this end he banishes unit designations from the language in which quantitative measurements are to be expressed, and devises a criterion of "empirical meaningfulness" in order to exclude (i) and its ilk. Very roughly, the criterion works as follows. The kinds of conventional choices we have to make in defining a numerical measure Fxn for a quantity q will determine the kinds of transformations which, when applied to Fxn, will produce another numerical measure for q. For example, if the choice of unit is sufficient to determine the numerical measure (as in the case of length and mass), then multiplication and/or addition by positive constants will preserve measurehood. In each case, measurement of the quantity is said to be invariant with respect to the type of transformations which preserve measurehood. Now a sentence of the unitless language is "empirically meaningful" (roughly) iff operating upon its measured quantities by a transformation with respect to which measurement of that quantity is invariant cannot change the truth-value of the sentence. Thus for (ii) to be meaningful, we must be able to multiply its measured quantities, viz. 'the mass of a' and 'the mass of b', by a positive constant without changing truth value. This is the case: (ii) is true iff 'm · (the mass of a) is greater than m · (the mass of b)' is true, for all m. The same holds for (iii). A sentence which fails this test is

(v)   The difference between the mass of a and the mass of b = 10.

Multiplication by a positive constant produces a sentence which is *incompatible* with (v), and hence that transformation cannot preserve truth-value. The same is true for (i), and it is *this* failing which determines its empirical meaninglessness for Suppes.

Suppes's approach appears to be strongly opposed to Ellis in its rejection of measurement sentences and its insistence that sentences such as (ii) and (iii) be analysed independently of the conditions under which numerical measures are defined. If we are persuaded that an account of measurement should start with quantitative relations unadulterated by convention, then the nominalization of Ellis's account of numerical measures seems beside the point. I think this appearance is mistaken. It is due to confusing two senses in which the analysis of (ii) and (iii) must be independent of numerical measures: (1) the analysis of (ii) and (iii) should not rest upon the *actual definition* of a numerical measure for mass; (2) the analysis of (ii) and (iii) should not rest upon the *analysis of the general conditions* under which a numerical measure for mass can be defined. (1) is undoubtedly correct, but (2) is more questionable: perhaps the "empirical meaning" of unitless sentences such as (ii) and (iii) rests upon the *general concept of unit*. That this is in fact the case may be seen from Suppes's own characterization of "empirical meaningfulness". For, that characterization presupposes that we have already isolated the kind of transformation which will preserve measurehood for the quantity in question. Only then can we operate upon the measured quantities of a sentence to check the invariance of its truth-value, and hence its "meaningfulness". As a result, the machinery developed in nominalizing Ellis's account is directly relevant to accommodating Suppes's account as well.

All that is needed is an analysis of the truth conditions of sentences like (ii) and (iii) which are "empirically meaningful" despite the lack of specific units—i.e., despite the lack of a particular numerical measure. Suppes's criterion gives us the key: their truth-value must be preserved by passing from one numerical measure to another; that is, their truth-value is independent of what numerical measure is chosen; that is, they are true for all numerical measures. Since (D2) already defines the notion of a numerical measure, all we need do is universally generalize. Thus (ii) becomes:

(ii)* (Fxn)(Fxn is a numerical measure for mass $\supset$ $\ulcorner$(m)(n)(Fam & Fbn) $\supset$ m>n$\urcorner$ holds).

In general, any sentence asserting a mathematical relation between measured quantities can be similarly transformed into a sentence asserting that the relation holds independently of the scale of measurement chosen for that quantity. Thus we can certainly express the sentences which Suppes regards as empirically fundamental without the prior conventional choice of numerical measure. The sentences which he regards as empirically "meaningless" will, if subjected to the same treatment, turn out false. For example, (i) becomes

(i)* (Fxn)(Fxn is a numerical measure for mass $\supset$ $\ulcorner$(m)(Fam $\supset$ m=4)$\urcorner$ holds)

which fails for some choices of Fxn. This does not mark a departure from Suppes's analysis, however. For, the falsity of (i)* is due precisely to the fact that (i) is sensitive to choice of unit, and hence what Suppes call meaninglessness becomes falsity on my analysis. What is important in Suppes's account is the distinction between those sentences whose truth is independent of convention and the others, and that the former are empirically fundamental. By generalizing with respect to numerical measure, the latter sentences become uniformly false precisely because they are sensitive to the choice of measure, while the former are free to be true or false as the facts dictate. Suppes may, if he chooses, decide to call this kind of falsity—i.e. falsity for this kind of reason—"empirical meaninglessness". Whether or not he does so, his contribution to the understanding of measurement is preserved. Thus the nominalization of Ellis's theory of measurement provides sufficient machinery to incorporate Suppes's approach as well.

Hilary Putnam has posed a general problem for a nominalist theory of measurement.[3] His argument has two phases.

The first phase consists of an appeal to a simple and natural way of defining distance. We start with the existence of space-time points and a physically significant relation of quadruples of them: C(x,y,z,w), which holds iff the interval xy is "congruent" to the interval zw (intuitively, the intervals are of equal length). We then choose two particular space-time points a and b and define the distance between them to be 1. Finally:

(D8)   The distance from x to y is r iff f(x,y) = r, where f is any function such that: (1) (v)(w)(f(v,w) has a non-negative real value); (2) (v)(w) (f(v,w) = 0 iff v = w); (3) (z)(u)(w)(f(z,u) = f(v,w) iff C(z,u,v,w)); (4) (u)(v)(w)((u,v,w, are colinear & v is between u and w) ⊃ (f(u,w) = f(u,v) + f(v,w))); and (5) f(a,b) = 1.

Putnam points out that, under reasonable conditions, it can be proved that there is a unique function satisfying (1)–(5), and hence distance is well defined. Putnam's conclusion from this example is: "... even if we take "points" as individuals, and the relation "C(x,y,z,w)" as primitive, still we cannot account for the numericalization of distance without quantifying over functions."

This argument has little weight. Notice that Putnam does not even attempt to *argue* that this is the *only* way to define distance. Hence he is not entitled to conclude "we *cannot* account ...". We saw above that at least one account of fundamental measurement, of which distance is an example, can be given without reference to numbers or functions. Furthermore, if we are given all the machinery that Putnam presupposes—space-time points *and line segments*, and the congruence relations—it is easy to formulate a simple nominalist definition, as follows:

(D9)   The distance from x to y = r (where r is an integer) iff there are exactly r colinear, continuous, non-overlapping intervals which together exhaust the interval xy, such that each is congruent to the interval ab.

(D10) The distance from x to y = r (where r is a proper fraction m/n) iff there are n pairwise congruent, colinear, continuous, non-overlapping intervals which together exhaust the inter-

[3] Putnam, 1971, chapter 4. 5

val ab, and such that a continuous sub-interval of ab composed of m of them is congruent to the interval xy.

Combining integers and fractions is trivial, hence all rational numbers are covered by (D9) and (D10).[4]

The second phase of Putnam's argument is much more difficult to deal with. He proves the following theorem for all nominalist languages—i.e., languages with a finite number of primitive predicates and singular terms whose quantifiers' domain consists of physical objects.

(T) For each n, let EXn be the sentence which says that exactly n things exist, and let L be a nominalist language. Then for each n we can find a set $\{S_1, S_2, \ldots, S_{i(n)}\}$ of sentences of L such that for any sentence S of L there is a j such that $\ulcorner Exn \supset (S \equiv S_j)\urcorner$ is logically true. (Equivalently, there is a finite partition $P_1, \ldots, P_{i(n)}$ of the sentences of L such that for all $j \leqslant i(n)$, if $S, S' \in P_j$ then $\ulcorner EXn \supset (S \equiv S')\urcorner$ is logically true.)

The significance of (T) is not easy to assess. It might be thought that since the sentences of L are partitioned into a finite set of equivalents, L is therefore barred from expressing an infinite number of different "facts" or relations among the members of the universe. But (T) by itself implies no such thing. For, the equivalence between the members of P_j is only *material* equivalence; thus *this* consequence of (T) is trivial: the sentences of any language are partitioned into two classes of material equivalents—the class of truths and the class of falsehoods. It might be thought that in the effectiveness of (T) ("we can find a set ...") lies its punch: since we can find $\{S_1, S_2, \ldots, S_{i(n)}\}$ and since we can effectively enumerate proofs, (T) guarantees that if the universe is finite we will be able to find some pairs of sentences which we will know to be materially equivalent merely by knowing that the universe has n members. But this result is also trivial: from EXn it certainly follows that there are such pairs of sentences—S and $\ulcorner S \&$ EXn$\urcorner$ for any S, for example.

Putnam attempts to use (T) to show that in a nominalist language intuitive logical relations among sentences must be misrepresented. Suppose we have a set Σ of sentences meeting the following

---

[4] Although Putnam's definition is expressed in terms of functions on real numbers and mine for rationals, Putnam concedes that rationals are all that can be *proven* necessary for science (at present), hence the nominalist cannot be defeated by the bare appeal to the real numbers.

conditions: (i) Σ is infinite; (ii) its members are pairwise logically independent; (iii) its members are pairwise incompatible, and thus no more than one member of Σ can be true (though this is not due to pure logic); and (iv) the truth-values of the members of Σ are independent of the size of the universe. Putnam claims that it follows from (T) that Σ cannot be expressed in a nominalist language. That this claim is correct may be seen as follows. Pick any n. Since Σ is infinite it must have members S and S' which are members of the same P_j; thus $\ulcorner EXn \supset (S \equiv S')\urcorner$ is a tautology. Now by (iii), since S and S' cannot both be true, $\ulcorner S \equiv S'\urcorner$ is true only if S and S' are both false. And so the truth values of two members of Σ are fixed solely by the size of the universe; this violates (iv), hence Σ is inexpressible. Since the material equivalences which undermine Σ are logical consequences of EXn, Putnam concludes that the fault lies in the incorrect representation of logical relations.

Of course, this result has interest only if we have reason to think that there are such sets Σ. This is the point at which (T) applies to the theory of measurement, since it is quite natural to think of sets of measurement sentences possessing characteristics (i)–(iv). As an example Putnam chooses the set {'x and y are (exactly) one metre apart', 'x and y are two metres apart', ..., 'x and y are n metres apart', ...}. This set is infinite and its members are logically independent. Its members are pairwise incompatible—x and y cannot be both (exactly) n metres apart and m meters apart where m $\neq$ n—though this incompatibility is not demonstrable formally.

And finally we do not see any reason for the size of the universe to fix the truth-values of any of the members of the set. If the universe contains exactly 100 entities, is there any limit to the number of different distance relations into which they can enter? It seems not. Putnam sums up the impact of (T) upon the theory of measurement by saying that a nominalist language cannot accommodate measurement sentences without distorting the logical relations among its sentences. For, via the argument of the last paragraph, (T) will guarantee that there are sentences 'x and y and r metres apart' and 'x and y are t metres apart' whose equivalence follows from EXn, even though their truth-values ought to be independent of the size of the universe. Therefore, Putnam concludes, a nominalist language is incapable in principle of expressing measurement sentences.

But Putnam is wrong. His argument is correct, but he has mis-understood its significance. This can be seen if we note that *none of the*

reasoning in the last three paragraphs—including the description of
(T)'s general impact and its application to measurement sentences—
made any appeal to L's being a nominalist language. Nor can the
proof of (T) itself require such an appeal, since what (T) shows is
that certain sentences are logically true, and the logical truth of a
sentence does not depend upon the domain assigned to its quantifiers.
Thus if the problem is, as Putnam says, one of unintuitive logical
relations, they cannot be avoided by changing the domain of the
quantifiers. And since it is only the domain of the quantifiers which
brands a language as nominalist, it follows that (T) applies across
the board to any first order language (with a finite primitive
vocabulary). If the problem described above is a problem at all, then it
is a problem for the concept of measurement itself, and not for the
ability of nominalist languages to express measurement sentences.

It may be objected that there are two separate problems here: (1)
the problem of unwanted logical relations which is indeed a problem
across the board for our philosophical account of measurement, and
specifically for finite-based, extensional languages to express measurement sentences in a philosophically acceptable way; (2) the problem of
using a finite-based extensional language to express sentences *without
risk of incorrect truth values.* Only nominalist languages are subject to
the radical failure of incorrect truth-values: if the universe is finite then
certain distance relations cannot be expressed by true sentences in
such a language. Platonist languages are not subject to such danger
since they provide an infinity of (abstract) entities.

The distinction between (1) and (2) may be admitted. But even
problem (2) will be misunderstood if it is cast as a choice between two
kinds of *language.* Choice of language is not the deciding factor; the
size of the universe is. To see this, consider the relative merits of the
following two languages, LP and LN. LP has all the usual vocabulary
of platonism: predicates and singular terms for numbers, functions,
properties, etc. LN has vocabulary for physical things only. In both
languages the quantifiers are understood to range over the entire
universe, i.e., the domain of all existing entities. (We assume that both
languages have finite primitive vocabulary.) Now *if the universe is
finite then* (2) *applies to LP and LN alike.* The extra vocabulary in LP
helps not at all unless an infinite universe of abstracta *exists* for that
vocabulary to describe. If the universe is infinite in its physical part,
then again there is no contrast between LP and LN: (2) fails to apply
to both. Only if the physical universe is finite and the abstract universe

infinite can a contrast be drawn for, although literally (2) will again fail to apply to both languages, the fact that all the primitive vocabulary of LN will apply only to a finite subset of the universe shows that the damaging result of (2) will still apply: LN will not have any sets of sentences meeting the conditions (i)–(iv).

Thus what Putnam is telling us is this: (a) measurement sentences form sets possessing (i)–(iv); (b) if the universe is finite then no language with a finite primitive vocabulary can express such sets of sentences; (c) we want finite-based languages and we want to express such sets of sentences; (d) therefore we should adopt a platonist language and the platonist assumption that there exist an infinity of abstract objects. There are three replies which can be made to this argument.

First, (a)–(d) is a development of problem (2); what about problem (1)? Even if we use LP and there are an infinity of abstracta, the logical relations described by (T) still hold in LP. Thus LP still verifies the conditional: if the universe is finite then no sets possessing (i)–(iv) are expressible. This itself shows that measurement sentences are not properly expressed in LP. Now a solution in problem (1) for LP requires a modification of LP which avoids the logical dependencies shown in (T). If the solution does not violate nominalist scruples, it could be grafted onto LN as well to avoid problem (2). In any case, since LP is not presently in the clear, the question of LN's adequacy to express measurement sentences cannot yet be decided.

Second, consider problem (2). Imagine using LN in a finite, wholly physical universe. LN misrepresents distance relations, we think, because the number of different distance relations which can obtain between the entities of that universe is not dependent upon how many things there are. Even if the universe consists of 25 electrons there may be an infinite number of different distance relations in which they can stand, and certainly cutting the number to 20 should not affect the number of those relations. The number of those relations is a brute physical fact about that universe. But if so, is it not incredible that platonism should affect this fact? Remember: merely adopting LP will not suffice; we need in addition to assume there exists an infinity of abstracta. Thus it appears that in a universe whose physical part is finite the number of distance relations which can obtain depends upon the existence of abstracta; as if the addition of abstracta makes the extra distance relations possible! Surely the existence of numbers, functions, and the like cannot bring about the existence of distance relations. Thus even if platonism (language plus assumption) escapes (T), it will not be *because of* platonism that problem (2) is avoided. And thus it is not *because* LN abjures abstracta that it faces problem (2). This strengthens the hope that whatever solves problem (2) for LP will do so as well for LN.

It may be objected that even though we need to assume the existence of an infinity of abstracta for LP to avoid problem (2), the point of this assumption is only to increase the descriptive power of LP. In a finite universe even LP is subject to (T), and what (T) says is that an infinity of mutually imcompatible states like distance relations cannot be expressed in LP. By assuming an infinite universe we avoid the material equivalences induced by EXn and hence can express such states. Thus the states themselves are given in the universe itself and not brought into being by the infinity assumption, but rather LP is made capable of describing them via this assumption. This objection is mistaken. To see why, consider the following representative case of the equivalences induced by EX2:

(*) $(\exists x)(\exists y)(z)(x \neq y \ \& \ (z=x \lor z=y)) \Rightarrow ((x)(x \text{ is red}) \equiv (\exists x)(\exists y)(x \neq y \ \& \ x \text{ is red} \ \& \ y \text{ is red})).$

The material equivalence which EX2 induces between

(1) $(x)(x \text{ is red})$

and

(2) $(\exists x)(\exists y)(x \neq y \ \& \ x \text{ is red} \ \& \ y \text{ is red})$

does not affect the content of those sentences – what they mean or express. They are logically, metaphysically, conceptually independent; they are independent in every interesting sense. What (*) shows is that *in a universe of exactly two entities* the same state of the universe determines the truth or falsity of both (1) and (2). If we add a third entity to the universe and thereby remove the material equivalence of (1) and (2), we do so *not* by affecting what they express but by adding to the states of the universe in such a way that different states are now responsible for the truth or falsity of (1) and (2). Thus the conclusion in the last paragraph is sustained: adding an infinity of abstracta to avoid (T) must be viewed by the platonist as *providing* the infinity of distance relations, and this is absurd.

Finally, some will wish to reply to Putnam by rejecting (a) of his argument. Notice that if measurement sentences are understood to satisfy (i)–(iv) by virtue of their meaning (i.e., satisfaction of (i)–(iv) is a criterion of correctness for the semantics of such sentences), then a philosophy of measurement such as Ellis's is ruled out. For, according to Ellis, measurement sentences describe the network of relations among entities which verify (D1)–(D7). If those relations do not obtain due to the finitude of the universe, Ellis will say that the measurable states do not obtain: not all the measurement sentences can be given truth conditions. (If true, this feature of measurement is similar to the relativity of motion: the latter guarantees that if there is only one entity in the universe, then there is no motion.) To assume that measurement sentences satisfy (i)–(iv) is to reject such a position by fiat. Thus as long as such a philosophy of measurement is in contention, Putnam's argument rests on an unsupported premiss.

We have seen so far that there is no reason to doubt the intrinsic ability of a nominalist language to express measurement sentences, and indeed, if Ellis's account of measurement is correct, we have seen how to express them. We must now check that the use of arithmetic with respect to measurement sentences will be properly represented by the account of arithmetic developed in chapter VI. Numerical measures (cf. (D2)) require that the order of a quantity be mirrored by the arithmetical order '<'. Arithmetic is applied in order to discover '<' relations and then draw conclusions concerning quantities, as in the following inference:

(*) (a) X weighs 5 lb
     (b) Y weighs 7 lb
     (c) Z weighs 10 lb
     (d) $(x)(y)$(weight of $\phi(x,y)$ = weight of x + weight of y)
     (e) $7 + 5 = 12$
     (f) Therefore, weight of $\phi(X,Y) = 12$ lb
     (g) $12 > 10$
     (h) Therefore, $\phi(X,Y)$ weighs more than Z.

(a)–(c) are given; (d) is an assumption concerning the particular numerical measure chosen for weight; (e) is guaranteed by arithmetic; (f) follows from (a)–(e) by logic; (h) follows from (c), (f), and (g) via (D2). The only question concerns the truth of (g). In chapter VI we saw that such sentences depend upon the size of the universe; in particular, (g) cannot be true unless there are at least 12 entities in the universe. Thus if we choose a numerical measure which assigns quantity values exceeding the size of the universe, we may find that the application of arithmetic to quantitative relations collapses. Do we need such numerical measures?

If we accept Ellis's account of measurement and we have a complete scale for weight, then the universe must be infinite. And even if the universe is finite, our ability to define a numerical scale depends upon the existence of a set of standards which builds step by step to match in weight the heaviest entity. We can always start numbering the standards with '1' and thus ensure that the numerical measure never exceeds the size of the universe. The same holds true, given Ellis's account, for fractions. We can employ a fractional weight m/n lb only if there are n standards equal in weight whose ϕ-combination is equal in weight to the first standard. Thus the fraction 'm/n' will be guaranteed application (cf. chapter VII). Since the arithmetic operations on fractions are defined so as to give standard truth-values for applicable fractions, the application of the arithmetic of fractions to measurement sentences will also be standard.

Appendix

Lemma 1: $(m)(n)((\exists F)(\exists!mxF \ \& \ \exists!nxF) \supset (F)(\exists!mxF \equiv \exists!nxF))$

Proof: Consider any instance of the Lemma. Either the numerals replacing 'm' and 'n' are identical, in which case the consequent is logically true; or they are different, in which the antecedent is logically false.

Lemma 2: Every numeral $\leqslant \bar{\bar{U}}$ has application.

Proof: Let $n \leqslant \bar{U}$. Then $(\exists x_1) \ldots (\exists x_n)\exists!nx(x=x_1 \vee \ldots \vee x=x_n)$.

Lemma 3: $n \neq n'$ iff 'n' has application.

Proof: $n \neq n'$ iff $(\exists F)(\exists!nxF \neq \exists!n'xF)$ iff $(\exists F)(\exists!nxF \vee \exists!n'F)$ (since '$\exists!nxF$' and '$\exists!n'xF$' are logically incompatible). Now $(\exists F)\exists!nxF$ iff 'n' has application, by definition. And $(\exists F)\exists!n'xF$ iff 'n' has application with respect to F as follows:

$$(\exists y)(Fy \ \& \ \exists!nx(Fx \ \& \ x \neq y)).$$

Lemma 4: All standardly true atomic sentences of AL0 are logically true.

Proof: Given in text of chapter VI (pp. 98–9).

Target Conditionals for Atomic Sentences of AL0

$a = b$: $(F)(\exists!axF \equiv \exists!bxF)$

I. If $\ulcorner a = b \urcorner$ is standardly true, then

$$(a \neq a' \ \& \ b \neq b') \supset a = b$$

is logically true.

Proof: Since the consequent is standardly true, it is logically true by Lemma 4; hence the whole is logically true.

II. If $\ulcorner a = b \urcorner$ is standardly false, then

$$(a \neq a' \ \& \ b \neq b') \supset a \neq b$$

is logically true.

Proof: Since $\ulcorner a \neq a' \urcorner$ holds, a has application, i.e. $\ulcorner (\exists F)\exists!axF \urcorner$ holds. But since $\ulcorner \exists!axF \urcorner$ and $\ulcorner \exists!bxF \urcorner$ are logically incompatible, $\ulcorner (\exists F)(\exists!axF \ \& \ \sim\exists!bxF) \urcorner$ holds, and then $\ulcorner a \neq b \urcorner$ follows.

Sabc: (F)(G) [(∃!axF & ∃!bxG & (x)~(F & G)) ⊃ ∃!cx(F ∨ G)]

I.   If ⌜Sabc⌝ is standardly true, then

$$c \neq c' \supset Sabc$$

is logically true.[1]

Proof: Since the consequent is standardly true, it is logically true by
            Lemma 4; hence the whole is logically true.

II.   If ⌜Sabc⌝ is standardly false, but ⌜Sabd⌝ is standardly true, then

$$d \neq d' \supset \sim Sabc$$

is logically true.[1]

Proof: The consequent is

(∃F)(∃G)[∃!axF & ∃!bxG & (x)~(F & G) & ~∃!cx(F ∨ G)].

Since the sum of a and b is not c, any pair of open sentences
which satisfies the first three conjuncts automatically satisfies the
fourth. Since ⌜d ≠ d'⌝ holds, it follows that $d \leqslant \overline{\overline{U}}$ and thus both a
and b have application. To satisfy the third conjunct we must
show that they have *disjoint* application. Since $d \leqslant \overline{\overline{U}}$ and d is the
sum of a and b, we may provide disjoint applications as follows:

(∃x₁) ... (∃x_d)[∃!ax(x=x₁ ∨ ... ∨ x=x_a) & ∃!bx(x=x_{a+1} ∨ ... ∨
x=x_d) & (x)~((x=x₁ ∨ ... ∨ x=x_a) & (x=x_{a+1} ∨ ... ∨ x=x_d))].

This is true if $x_1, ..., x_d$ are different elements of U.

PObc: S00c
Pa'bc: (∃d)(Pabd & Sdbc)

I.   If ⌜Pabc⌝ is standardly true, then

$$c \neq c' \supset Pabc$$

is logically true.[1]

Proof: Since the consequent is standardly true, it is logically true; thus
            the whole is logically true.

II.   If ⌜Pabc⌝ is standardly false, but ⌜Pabd⌝ is standardly true, then

$$d \neq d' \supset \sim Pabc$$

is logically true.[1]

Proof: (i) If a is '0' then the truth condition of the consequent is ⌜~S00c.⌝
            Since a·b ≠ c, c is not '0' and so ⌜S00c⌝ is not standardly true.
            Thus its negation follows from ⌜d ≠ d'⌝.
            (ii) If a is not '0', then the truth condition of the consequent
            starts with a string of additions which are generalizations of
            standard truths and ends with an addition which is standardly

[1] The expression of applicability in the antecedent is equivalent to the formulation
in chapter VI.

false. $\ulcorner d \neq d'\urcorner$ guarantees that all the additions have application, hence the negation of the last addition (and hence the whole conjunction) follows from $\ulcorner d \neq d'\;\urcorner$. For example, the truth condition for $\ulcorner P0'''0''c\urcorner$ is

$$(\exists e)(\exists f)(\exists g)(S00g \;\&\; Sg0''f \;\&\; Sf0''e \;\&\; Se0''c).$$

Since d is $0''''''$, $\ulcorner d \neq d'\urcorner$ guarantees the applicability of $0 + 0$, $0 + 0''$, $0'' + 0''$ and $0'''' + 0''$, thus g, f, and e are unambiguously determined as 0, $0''$, and $0''''$ respectively. Now c is *not* $0''''''$, hence $\ulcorner S0''''0''c\urcorner$ is standardly false. Its negation thus follows from the applicability of $0'''' + 0''$ which is given by $\ulcorner d \neq d'\urcorner$.

Proofs of the Logical Truths of the Axioms

$(n)(0 \neq n')$

Proof: Let a be any numeral. Then $\ulcorner \exists!0xF\urcorner$ and $\ulcorner \exists a'F\urcorner$ are logically incompatible, so $\ulcorner (F)(\exists!0xF \equiv \exists!a'F)\urcorner$ is logically false,[2] and so $\ulcorner \sim(F)(\exists!0xF \equiv \exists!a'F)\urcorner$ is logically true. Thus all instances of A1 are logically true. (I am assuming that L has at least one predicate.)

$(m)(n)(((m' \neq m'' \lor n' \neq n'') \;\&\; m'=n') \supset m=n)$

Proof:
(1) $m' \neq m''$, i.e. $(\exists F)(\exists!m'xF \not\equiv \exists!m''xF)$ hyp
(2) $m' = n'$, i.e. $(F)(\exists!m'xF \equiv \exists!n'xF)$ hyp
(3) $(\exists F)\exists!m'xF \lor (\exists F)\exists!m''xF$ (1)
(4) $(\exists F)\exists!m'xF \supset (\exists F)\exists!n'xF$ (2)
(5) $(\exists F)\exists!m''xF \supset (\exists y)(\exists F)\exists!m'x(F \;\&\; x \neq y)$ (R1), (R2), logic
(6) $(\exists y)(\exists F)\exists!m'x(F \;\&\; x \neq y)$
     $\supset (\exists y)(\exists F)\exists!n'x(F \;\&\; x \neq y)$ (2), (R1), (R2)
(7) $(\exists F)\exists!n'xF \lor (\exists y)(\exists F)\exists!n'(F \;\&\; x \neq y)$ (3)–(6), logic
(8) $\exists!nxG$ hyp
(9) $(\exists y)(\sim(\exists x)(x=y \;\&\; G)$
     $\&\; \exists!n'x(G \lor x=y))$ (7), (8), logic
(10) $(\exists y)(\sim(\exists x)(x=y \;\&\; G) \;\&\; \exists!m'x(G \lor x=y))$ (2), (9)
(11) $\exists!mxG$ (10), logic
(12) $(G)(\exists!nxG \supset \exists!mxG)$ conditionalization of (8) and (10), gen
(13) $\exists!mxG$ hyp
(14) $(\exists y)(\sim(\exists x)(x=y \;\&\; G) \;\&\; \exists!m'x(G \lor x=y))$ (3), (13), logic
(15) $(\exists y)(\sim(\exists x)(x=y \;\&\; G) \;\&\; \exists!n'x(G \lor x=y))$ (2), (14)
(16) $\exists!nxG$ (15), logic
(17) $(G)(\exists!mxG \supset \exists!nxG)$ conditionalization of (13) and (16), gen
(18) $m = n$ (12), (17)

[2] Let F be '$x \neq x$'.

(n)Sn0n

Proof: The truth condition for this axiom is

$$(n)(F)(G)((∃!nxF \ \& \ ∃!0xG \ \& \ {\sim}(∃x)(F \ \& \ G)) ⊃ ∃!nx(F ∨ G)$$

which is an obvious tautology when instances are provided their truth conditions.

(m)(n)(r)(Smnr ⊃ Sm′nr′)

Proof: (1)   Smnr, i.e. (F)(G)((∃!mxF & ∃!nxG & ~(∃x)(F & G)) ⊃
                  ∃!rx(F ∨ G)) hyp

           (2)   ∃!m′xH & ∃!nxJ & ~(∃x)(H & J) hyp

           (3)   (∃y)((∃x)(x=y & H) & ∃!mx(H & x≠y) & ∃!nxJ &
                  ~(∃x)(H & x≠y & J)) (2), logic, 'y' assumed not to be free
                  in (2)

           (4)   (∃y)((∃x)(x=y & H) & ∃!r((H & x≠y) ∨ J)) (1), (3)

           (5)   (r)(F)(y)((∃!rxF & ~(∃x)(x=y & F)) ⊃ ∃!r′x(F ∨ x=y))
                  logic

           (6)   (∃y)((∃x)(x=y & H)) & ∃!r′x(((H & x≠y) ∨ J) ∨ x=y) (2),
                  (4), (5), logic

           (7)   (∃y)((∃x)(x=y & H) & ∃!r′x(H ∨ J ∨ x=y)) (6), logic

           (8)   (∃y)((∃x)(x=y & H) & ∃!r′x (H ∨ J)) (7), logic

           (9)   ∃!r′x (H ∨ J) (8)

          (10)   Sm′rn′ conditionalization of (2) and (9), gen

(m)(n)(r)(((∃t)~Sm′nt & Sm′nr′) ⊃ Smnr)

Proof: (1)   (∃t)~Sm′nt, i.e. (∃t)(∃F)(∃G)(∃!m′xF & ∃!nxG &
                  ~(∃x)(F & G) & ~∃!tx(F ∨ G)) hyp

           (2)   Sm′nr′, i.e. (F)(G)((∃!m′xF & ∃!nxG & ~(∃x)(F & G)) ⊃
                  ∃!r′x(F ∨ G)) hyp

           (3)   ∃!mxH & ∃!nxJ & ~(∃x)(H & J) hyp

           (4)   (∃y)(∃!m′x(H ∨ x=y) & ∃!nxJ & ~(∃x)((H ∨ x=y) & J))
                  (1),(3), logic

           (5)   ∃!r′x(H ∨ x=y ∨ J) (2),(4)

           (6)   ∃!rx(H ∨ J) (5), logic

           (7)   Smnr conditionalization of (2) and (6), gen.

(n) Pn00

Proof: The truth condition for this axiom is ⌜S000⌝ which is logically
           true.

(m)(n)(r)[Pmn′r ≡ (∃s)(Pmns & Smsr)]

Proof: The truth condition for ⌜Pab′c⌝ makes this an immediate
           tautology.

[...0...& (n)(...n...⊃...n′...)] ⊃ (n)...n...

Proof: The antecedent guarantees that each of ⌜...0...⌝, ⌜...0′...⌝,
           ⌜...0″...,⌝ —— will be true, and by the substitutional

semantics for '(n)' the consequent will then also be true. Hence any substitutional interpretation for AL0 which makes the antecedent true does likewise for the consequent: A8 is true in all interpretations, i.e., logically true. Note that this is only a proof that (each instance of) A8 is logically true; it is not a "justification of induction", hence the use of induction in the metalanguage is unobjectionable.

$(m)(n)[m=n \supset (\ldots m \ldots \supset \ldots n \ldots)]$

Proof: In all the truth conditions for sentences of AL0, the immediate context for all numerals is '∃!—x'. Since $\ulcorner a = b \urcorner$ guarantees material equivalence for all such contexts, substitution of a for b in any sentence of AL0 cannot affect truth-value.

Target Conditionals for Definitions in Arithmetic

$a<b =df (\exists n)(Sanb \ \& \ (\exists m)\sim Sanm \ \& \ n \neq 0)$

I.   If $\ulcorner a < b \urcorner$ is standardly true, then

$$(a \neq a' \ \& \ b \neq b') \supset a<b$$

is logically true.

Proof: Since a is less than b, let $a+c = b$, $c \neq 0$. Then $\ulcorner Sacb \urcorner$ is standardly true, and hence logically true; and since c is less than b and b has application, c also has application, and thus $\ulcorner c \neq 0 \urcorner$ is logically true. Finally, since $a + c$ has application, $\ulcorner Sacd \urcorner$ will be true iff standardly true, and hence sometimes false. Thus we have

$$Sacb \ \& \ \sim Sacd \ \& \ c \neq 0$$

follows from $\ulcorner b \neq b \urcorner$, and I follows by generalization on c and d.

II. If $\ulcorner a<b \urcorner$ is standardly false, then

$$(a \neq a' \ \& \ b \neq b') \supset \sim(a<b)$$

is logically true.

Proof: The consequent is:

$$(n)((Sanb \ \& \ n \neq 0) \supset (m)Sanm).$$

Since a is not less than b, $\ulcorner Sacb \ \& \ c \neq 0 \urcorner$ is true only if $a + c$ is not applicable, and in that case $\ulcorner Sacd \urcorner$ will be true for any d.

$a/b =df (\exists n)(Panb \ \& \ (\exists m)\sim Panm \ \& \ n \neq 0)$

I.   If $\ulcorner a/b \urcorner$ is standardly true, then

$$(a \neq a' \ \& \ b \neq b') \supset a/b$$

is logically true.

Proof: Since a divides b, a·c = b for some c ≠ 0, and so $\ulcorner$Pacb$\urcorner$ is standardly true and thus logically true. Since b has application and c is less than b, c has application; thus $\ulcorner$c ≠ 0$\urcorner$ follows from $\ulcorner$b ≠ b′$\urcorner$. Since a·c has application, the truth-value of $\ulcorner$Pacd$\urcorner$ will be standard for all d, and thus its falsity for all but one d follows from $\ulcorner$b ≠ b′$\urcorner$. So we can choose c and d so that

$$Pacb \ \& \sim Pacd \ \& \ c \neq 0$$

follows from $\ulcorner$b ≠ b′$\urcorner$. I follows by generalization.

II.   If $\ulcorner$a/b$\urcorner$ is standardly false, then

$$(a \neq a' \ \& \ b \neq b') \supset \sim(a/b)$$

is logically true.

Proof: The consequent is

$$(n)[(Panb \ \& \ n \neq 0) \supset (m)Panm].$$

Since a does not divide b, no choice of c makes $\ulcorner$Pacb & c≠0$\urcorner$ standardly true. Thus $\ulcorner$Pacb & c≠0$\urcorner$ is true only if a·c has no application, and in that case $\ulcorner$Pacd$\urcorner$ will be true for all d.

E(a,0,c): c = 0′
E(a,b′,c): (∃d)(E(a,b,d) & Padc)

I.   If $\ulcorner$E(a,b,c)$\urcorner$ is standardly true, then

$$c \neq c \supset E(a,b,c)$$

is logically true.

II.   If $\ulcorner$E(a,b,c)$\urcorner$ is standardly false, but $\ulcorner$E(a,b,d)$\urcorner$ is standardly true, then

$$d \neq d' \supset \sim E(a,b,c)$$

is logically true.

Proofs: Analogous to multiplication.

Target Conditionals for Arithmetic of Fractions

a/b == c/d =df (∃n)[(Panc & (∃m)∼Panm & Pbnd & (∃m)∼Pbdm)

$\qquad\qquad$ ∨ (Pcna & (∃m)∼Pcnm & Pdnb & (∃m)∼Pdnm)]

a/b = c/d = df (∃r)(∃s)((r/s == a/b) & (r/s == c/d))

I.   If $\ulcorner$a/b = c/d$\urcorner$ is standardly true, then

$$(b \neq b' \ \& \ d \neq d') \supset (a/b = c/d)$$

is logically true.

Proof: Since $\ulcorner$a/b = c/d$\urcorner$ is standardly true, either one fraction is reducible to the other, or they are both reducible to a third.

Assume the former (the proof to follow can easily be adapted to the latter), and let $\ulcorner a/b \urcorner$ be reducible to $\ulcorner c/d \urcorner$ via e, i.e., $\ulcorner Pcea \urcorner$ and $\ulcorner Pdeb \urcorner$ are standardly true, and hence tautologies. Furthermore, since $\ulcorner b \neq b' \urcorner$ holds, $b \leqslant \overline{\overline{U}}$; and so the truth-value of Pdef will agree with its standard truth-value, hence $(\exists m){\sim}$Pdem holds. That is, $b \neq b'$ logically implies $\ulcorner (\exists m){\sim}\text{Pdem} \urcorner$. Since the fractions are proper, and all numerals $\leqslant U$ have application, $\ulcorner a \neq a' \urcorner$ holds, and thus $\ulcorner (\exists m){\sim}\text{Pcem} \urcorner$ follows as well. Thus we have

$$b \neq b' \supset (a/b == c/d)$$

is logically true. Since

$$(a/b == c/d) \supset (a/b = c/d)$$

is also logically true, I is proved.

II.   If $\ulcorner a/b = c/d \urcorner$ is standardly false, then

$$(b \neq b' \ \& \ d \neq d') \supset (a/b \neq c/d)$$

is logically true.

Proof: I will show that

$$(b \neq b' \ \& \ d \neq d') \supset {\sim}(a/b == c/d)$$

is logically true; the application to $\ulcorner a/b \neq c/d \urcorner$ is obvious. Now the consequent is:

$$(n)[\{((\exists m){\sim}\text{Panm} \ \& \ (\exists m){\sim}\text{Pbnm}) \supset {\sim}(\text{Panc} \ \& \ \text{Pbnd})\}$$
$$\& \ \{((\exists m){\sim}\text{Pcnm} \ \& \ (\exists m){\sim}\text{Pdnm}) \supset {\sim}(\text{Pcna} \ \& \ \text{Pdnb})\}].$$

In each $\{\}$-clause the consequent says that one of $\ulcorner a/b \urcorner$, $\ulcorner c/d \urcorner$ cannot be reduced to the other via n, and the antecedent says that the multiplications which establish the reduction are unique. Now since $\ulcorner a/b = c/d \urcorner$ is standardly false, $\ulcorner a/b \urcorner$ and $\ulcorner c/d \urcorner$ are not reducible one to the other, thus the consequents of the $\{\}$-clauses must be standardly true *if* the reducing multiplications are unique; and *that* is guaranteed by the antecedent. Hence the $\{\}$-clauses are logically true, and thus the consequent of II is logically true, which makes II logically true.

$$s(a/b, c/d, e/f) =df (\exists m)(\exists n)(\exists s)(\exists f)(\text{Pnbf} \ \& \ (\exists r){\sim}\text{Pnbr} \ \& \ \text{Pmdf}$$
$$\& \ (\exists r){\sim}\text{Pmdr} \ \& \ \text{Pnas} \ \& \ (\exists r){\sim}\text{Pnar} \ \& \ \text{Pmct}$$
$$\& \ (\exists r){\sim}\text{Pmcr} \ \& \ \text{Sste} \ \& \ (\exists r){\sim}\text{Sstr})$$
$$S(a/b, c/d, e/f) =df (\exists r)(\exists s)(\exists t)(\exists u)(\exists v)((r/s = a/b) \ \& \ (t/u = c/d) \ \& \ L(r/s)$$
$$\& \ L(t/u) \ \& \ s(r/s, t/u, v/w) \ \& \ (v/w = e/f))$$

I.   If $\ulcorner S(a/b, c/d, e/f) \urcorner$ is standardly true, then

$$(b{\neq}b' \ \& \ d{\neq}d' \ \& \ f{\neq}f') \supset S(a/b, c/d, e/f)$$

is logically true.

Proof: Taking e and f as substituends for 'r' and 's' respectively, the multiplications and additions in the definiens of the consequent are all standardly true, and hence logically true.

II.   If $\ulcorner S(a/b, c/d, e/f) \urcorner$ is standardly false, but $S(a/b, c/d, g/h)$ is standardly true, then

$$(b{\neq}b' \ \& \ d{\neq}d' \ \& \ h{\neq}h') \supset {\sim}S(a/b, c/d, e/f)$$

is logically true.

Proof: Since the sum of $\ulcorner a/b \urcorner$ and $\ulcorner c/d \urcorner$ is not $\ulcorner e/f \urcorner$, not all the additions and multiplications in the definiens of $\ulcorner S(a/b, c/d, e/f) \urcorner$ are standardly true; their falsity follows from the antecedent which guarantees that they all have application. Hence the conditional is logically true.

$p(a/b, c/d, e/f) =_{df} Pace \ \& \ (\exists r){\sim}Pacr \ \& \ Pbdf \ \& \ (\exists r){\sim}Pbdf$

$P(a/b, c/d, e/f) =_{df} (\exists r)(\exists s)(\exists t)(\exists u)(\exists v)(\exists w)((r/s = a/b) \ \& \ (t/u = c/d)$

$\qquad \& \ L(r/s) \ \& \ L(t/u) \ \& \ L(r/u) \ \& \ L(t/s) \ \& \ p(r/s, t/u, v/w)$

$\qquad \& \ (v/w = e/f))$

I.   If $\ulcorner P(a/b, c/d, e/f) \urcorner$ is standardly true, then

$$(b{\neq}b' \ \& \ d{\neq}d' \ \& \ f{\neq}f') \supset P(a/b, c/d, e/f)$$

is logically true.

II.   If $P(a/b, c/d, e/f)$ is standardly false, but '$P(a/b, c/d, g/h)$' is standardly true, then

$$(b{\neq}b' \ \& \ d{\neq}d' \ \& \ h{\neq}h') \supset {\sim}P(a/b, c/d, e/f)$$

is logically true.

Proofs: Analogous to addition.

References

[1] Benaceraff, Paul, "Mathematical Truth", *Journal of Philosophy*, 70 (1973), pp. 661–79.

[2] Boolos, George, "On Second Order Logic", *Journal of Philosophy*, 72 (1975), pp. 509–27.

[3] Cartwright, Richard, "Ontology and the Theory of Meaning", *Philosophy of Science*, 21 (1954), pp. 316–25.

[4] Chihara, Charles, *Ontology and the Vicious Circle Principle*, Ithaca and London: Cornell University Press, 1973.

[5] Davidson, Donald, "Theories of Meaning and Learnable Languages", in Y. Bar-Hillel, ed., *Logic, Methodology and Philosophy of Science, Proceedings of the 1964 International Congress*, Amsterdam: North-Holland, 1965, pp. 383–94.

[6] ——, "Truth and Meaning", *Synthese*, 17 (1967), pp. 304–23.

[7] ——, "The Logical Form of Action Sentences", in N. Rescher, ed., *The Logic of Decision and Action*, Pittsburgh: University of Pittsburgh Press, 1967, pp. 81–95.

[8] ——, "Semantics for Natural Languages", *Linguaggi nella Societa e nella Tecnica*, Milan, 1970, pp. 177–88.

[9] ——, "In Defense of Convention T", in [29], pp. 76–86.

[10] ——, "The Method of Truth in Metaphysics", *Midwest Studies in Philosophy*, 2 (1977), pp. 244–54.

[11] Dummett, Michael, *Frege: Philosophy of Language*, New York: Harper and Row, 1973.

[12] Dunn, Michael and Belnap, Nuel, "The Substitution Interpretation of the Quantifiers", *Nous*, 2 (1968), pp. 177–85.

[13] Ellis, Brian, *Basic Concepts of Measurement*, Cambridge: Cambridge University Press, 1968.

[14] Fefferman, Solomon, "Systems of Predicative Analysis", *Journal of Symbolic Logic*, 29 (1964), pp. 1–30.

[15] Field, Hartry, "Tarski's Theory of Truth", *Journal of Philosophy*, 69 (1972), pp. 347–74.

[16] Fodor, Jerry, "Troubles about Actions", in D. Davidson and G. Harman, eds., *Semantics of Natural Language*, Dordrecht: Reidel, 1972, pp. 25–48.

[17] van Fraassen, Bas, *Formal Semantics and Logic*, New York: Macmillan, 1971.

[18] Goodman, Nelson, *Languages of Art*, Indianapolis: Hackett, 1976.

[19] Gottlieb, Dale, "Foundations of Logical Theory", *American Philosophical Quarterly*, 11 (1974), pp. 337–43.

[20] ——, "Reference and Ontology", *Journal of Philosophy*, 17 (1974), pp. 587–99.

[21] ——, "A Method for Ontology, with Applications to Numbers and Events", *Journal of Philosophy*, 73 (1976), pp. 637–51.

[22] ——, "The Truth About Arithmetic", *American Philosophical Quarterly*, 15 (1978), pp. 81–90.

[23] Gottlieb, Dale, and McCarthy, Timothy, "Substitutional Quantification and Set Theory", *Journal of Philosophical Logic*, 1979.

[24] Jubien, Michael, "The Intensionality of Ontological Commitment", *Nous*, 6 (1972), pp. 378–87.

[25] ——, "Ontological Commitment to Particulars", *Synthese*, 28 (1974), pp. 513–32.

[26] ——, "Ontology and Mathematical Truth," *Nous*, 11 (1977), pp. 133–50.

[27] Kripke, Saul, "Naming and Necessity", in D. Davidson and G. Harman, eds., *Semantics of Natural Language*, Dordrecht: Reidel, 1972, pp. 253–355.

[28] ——, "Is There a Problem about Substitutional Quantification?" in Evans and McDowell, eds., *Truth and Meaning*, Oxford: Clarendon Press, 1976, pp. 325–419.

[29] Leblanc, Hughes, ed., *Truth, Syntax and Modality*, Amsterdam: North-Holland, 1973.

[30] Marcus, Ruth Barcan, "Modalities and Intensional Languages", in Marx Wartofsky, ed., *Studies in the Philosophy of Science*, Dordrecht: Reidel, 1963, pp. 77–96.

[31] ——, "Quantification and Ontology", *Nous*, 6 (1972), pp. 240–50.

[32] Oliver, J. W., "Ontic Content and Commitment", in R. Severns, ed., *Ontological Commitment*, Athens, Ga.: University of Georgia Press, 1974, pp. 91–104.

[33] Parsons, Charles, "A Plea for Substitutional Quantification", *Journal of Philosophy*, 68 (1971), pp. 231–7.

[34] ——, "Ontology and Mathematics", *Philosophical Review*, 80 (1971), pp. 151–76.

[35] ——, "Sets and Classes", *Nous*, 8 (1974), pp. 1–12.

[36] Putnam, Hilary, *Philosophy of Logic*, New York: Harper and Row, 1971.

[37] Quine, W. V. O., "Designation and Existence", *Journal of Philosophy*, 36 (1939), pp. 701–9.

[38] ——, *Word and Object*, Cambridge, Mass.: MIT Press, 1960.

[39] ——, *From a Logical Point of View*, Cambridge, Mass.: Harvard University Press, 1961.

[40] ——, *Ontological Relativity and Other Essays*, New York: Columbia University Press, 1968.

[41] ——, "Existence and Quantification", in *Ontological Relativity and Other Essays*, New York, Columbia University Press, 1968, pp. 151–64.

[42] ——, *The Roots of Reference*, La Salle: Open Court, 1973.

[43] ——, *Philosophy of Logic*, Englewood: Prentice-Hall, 1973.

[44] Scheffler, Israel and Chomsky, Noam, "What is Said to Be", *Proceedings of the Aristotelian Society*, 59 (1958–9), pp. 71–82.

[45] Suppes, P., "Measurement, Empirical Meaningfulness and Three-Valued Logic", in Churchman and Ratoosh, eds., *Measurement: Definition and Theories*, New York: Wiley, 1959, pp. 129–43.

[46] Suppes, P. and Zinnes, J., "Basic Measurement Theory", in Luce, Bush, Galanter, eds., *Handbook of Mathematical Psychology*, New York: Wiley, 1963.

[47] Wang, Hao, *A Survey of Mathematical Logic*, Amsterdam: North-Holland, 1962.

Index